Bringing Churches Together

BRINGING CHURCHES TOGETHER

AN INTRODUCTION TO
ECUMENISM

GIDEON ◆ GOOSEN

E. J. DWYER

First published in 1993 by
E. J. Dwyer (Australia) Pty Ltd
3/32-72 Alice Street
Newtown NSW 2042
Australia
Phone: (02) 550-2355
Fax: (02) 519-3218

National Library of Australia
Cataloguing-in-Publication data

Goosen, Gideon C.
   Bringing churches together.
   Bibliography.
   Includes index.
   ISBN 0 85574 173 2.
   1. Ecumenical movement. 2. Christian union. I. Title.
270.82

Nihil Obstat: Rev. Richard Lennan, B.A.(Hons),S.T.B.,
M.Phil(OXon),D.Theol(Innsbruck).
Censor Deputatus.

Imprimatur: Bishop Bede Heather, D.D.,L.S.S.
Diocese of Parramatta.

The *Nihil Obstat* and *Imprimatur* are official declarations that the work
contains nothing contrary to Faith or Morals. It is not implied thereby that
those granting the *Nihil Obstat* and *Imprimatur* agree with the contents,
statements, or opinions expressed.

Distributed in Ireland and the UK by:
   Columba Book Service
   93 The Rise
   Mount Merrion
   BLACKROCK CO. DUBLIN
   Ph: (01) 283 2954
   Fax: (01) 288 3770

Cover design & illustration by Todd Davidson
Edited by Kevin Mark
Text designed by Katrina Rendell
Typeset in Galliard 11/13pt by ACP Colour Graphics, Sydney

Table of Contents

Illustrations, Maps, Charts and Tables

ACKNOWLEDGEMENTS

There are a number of people who, in one way or another, have helped in the realization of this book. I would like to thank those who read sections of the manuscript: Mrs Margie Beck, Rev. Dr John Chryssavgis, Rev. David Gill, Dr Malcolm Prentis, Fr Michael Putney, Ms Denise Sullivan and Rev. Dr Ray Williamson. My thanks also go to Archbishop Mar T. Aboodi, Bishops Balliozian and Mar Meelis Zaia and Frs M. Tawfik, M. Nemetalla and P. Skariah for their help with the Oriental Churches. I am grateful too, to those who encouraged this project in various ways: Mr Graham English, Dr Chris Harris, Dr Charles Hill, Fr Edward Yarnold and Mr Nicholas Vidot. In addition to the above, I owe a special thanks to the staff of the Australian Council of Churches and the New South Wales Ecumenical Council in Sydney who have been most cooperative in allowing me to use their resources; and to Miss Lynette Champion for invaluable help in the ACU Library.

DEDICATION

I would like to dedicate this book to all those people who have been part of my ongoing ecumenical journey: to my extended family, especially my wife, Caroline; to the Glenbrook Inter-Church prayer-group, of which I am privileged to be a member; to all my students; and to those invited speakers from different religious traditions who have always been willing to share their knowledge and insights with others.

Introduction

This book is an introduction to ecumenism. It is for the general reader or student of theology who would like to be better informed about ecumenism. It covers both the theological and historical aspects of ecumenism because I believe that they are inextricably linked. It takes in the theology of ecumenism, current dialogues and issues, the history of the World Council of Churches and the two main rifts in Christianity, namely the schism between East and West in the eleventh century and the Protestant Reformation in the sixteenth century.

Important figures of the Reformation period, such as Luther, Calvin, Zwingli and Henry VIII, are sketched to fill out the story. Historical background is essential as it highlights and contextualizes the issues at stake between the relevant religious traditions. These issues are central to any contemporary dialogue. Without an understanding of these issues, progress in discussions will be difficult, if not impossible. It has often been said that in order to understand the present, and move confidently into the future, one must have an appreciation of the past. It is my experience that, for one reason or another, this understanding and knowledge of historical background is often lacking.

For those who would like to pursue the historical detail of the rifts in general or individuals in particular, a selective reading list is given at the end of Chapters Three and Four.

Some important issues that emerge from current discussions are examined at close quarters in Chapter Five. The ecumenical issues selected for discussion, while not being exhaustive in scope, are critical for further progress and sooner or later the churches are going to have to deal seriously with them. By way of update, the present situation regarding the busy world of international ecumenical dialogues is given in Chapter Six. But it is more than that, for in looking at the dialogues and the issues they raise, other aspects are revealed about the interests, theologies and past hurts sustained by different churches.

Finally, Appendices B to E provide easily accessible information about the historical side of ecumenism which are a useful supplement to the early chapters. A glossary is given which will help with new or technical terms. Sources for further readings are indicated both in endnotes and in the bibliography.

Ecumenism is a living movement, not a museum piece. Chapter Seven describes practical ways in which an ordinary individual can promote ecumenism. It is my hope that this book, as well as being informative, will encourage readers to take up some of these suggestions and become actively involved at the local level in the process of ecumenism. Should this happen the book will have been a worthwhile project.

Each chapter ends with a number of discussion questions which are designed to pick up points raised in that particular chapter and, where possible, to tap into individuals' life experiences. Listening to another's experience can be a very profound way of learning, and as a means of education in ecumenism should not be underestimated.

Although the discussion questions are obviously written with a verbal discussion in mind, most of them could also be used for a written exercise, journal writing, or assignment, depending on how this book is being used.

Appendix A, entitled, 'Activities for Further Ecumenical Learning', provides a number of practical suggestions for experiential learning in the area of ecumenism and caters for a variety of ages from young adults upwards.

CHAPTER ONE

The Theology of Ecumenism

Today's world is torn apart in many ways. One instinctively thinks of the ongoing wounds that are inflicted on humanity in places like Northern Ireland and the Middle East with a relentlessness that sometimes leads to despair. On the other hand, we have witnessed in recent times the remarkable changes that have occurred in places like Eastern Europe and South Africa. We have seen the overthrow of communism and the rejection of apartheid. These events are surely inspirational and significant in that they prove that change is possible and that the wounds inflicted by the injustices of individuals or regimes can be healed.

Ecumenism is all about healing wounds. Its basic meaning is simple—it refers to the movement towards restoring unity among Christian churches. The sad reality is that Christianity is split into three main groups as the following pie-chart shows:[1]

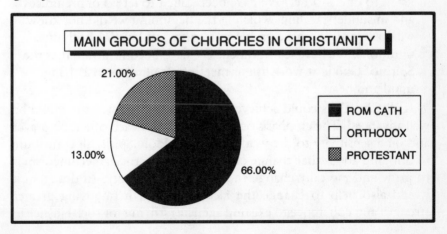

MAIN GROUPS OF CHURCHES IN CHRISTIANITY

21.00%

13.00%

66.00%

■ ROM CATH
□ ORTHODOX
▨ PROTESTANT

However within these groups there are further divisions as the chart on page 28 clearly shows. For too long Christian churches have perpetuated these divisions by fighting among themselves or simply maintaining the status quo. Now they have been bold and courageous enough to call a halt to the hatred and simultaneously taken steps to improve their relationships with each other.

Sometimes people may associate the word 'ecumenism' with meetings of church leaders and the almost inevitable subsequent 'agreed statements', 'reports' or 'declarations', whose contents often seem quite far removed from one's daily life. More often than not, the people in the pews do not even get to hear about the existence of these statements. Without undervaluing the importance of these statements, ecumenism is, in the first instance, more concerned with people than with paper.

The heart of the matter

In the foreword to one of these statements there is a very significant paragraph about the dynamics which come into play when ecumenism is at work and which touches the very heart of the matter. I will let the document speak for itself. It arose out of a Lutheran-Roman Catholic dialogue. The relevant passage reads as follows:

> We have met each other at depth. We have been built up by each other's faith in Jesus Christ. We have been challenged truly to listen to one another. We have been called to let go of prejudices and misunderstandings which in the beginning we did not know we possessed. We have grown in respect and love for both our traditions. We have learnt much. We have become aware that the Spirit of God is at work in our meetings, calling us to a change of mind and heart.[2]

If all Christians could achieve these insights, ecumenism would be well advanced! The emphasis on getting to know each other, on prayer and on a sensitivity to the workings of the Holy Spirit, all contribute to bringing about that change of heart which is crucial if ecumenism is to grow and radically change the face of Christianity. In doing so it would also help to change the face of the earth by giving greater strength and coherence to existing agencies striving for social justice in so many areas—nuclear disarmament, poverty, Third World debt, environmental issues and denial of human rights.

One of the modern saints who illustrates this spirit, this change of heart, is Brother Roger Schutz of Taizé fame. He came from a Reformed Church background, but a period of living with a French Catholic family while he was an adolescent and the example of his grandmother had a positive ecumenical influence on the rest of his life.[3] The community that he founded in the small village of Taizé, France, during the Second World War was small and had simple rules. One aim was to promote reconciliation between people, especially Christian churches. He was particularly devoted to youth. One of his inspirations, the Council of Youth, which opened in 1974, attracts thousands of young people to Taizé every year. Pope John Paul II commented that on the journey of life Taizé is like a spring where one stops, refreshes oneself, and then continues.

In his simplicity and holiness Brother Roger became friends with another great ecumenist, Pope John XXIII, whom he used to see once a year. Not surprisingly he is also a friend of Mother Theresa of Calcutta. His love for people and young people in particular, is boundless. Once, when asked how he lived, he said he tried to bring as much love as possible to every moment, every action in his day. The woundedness of humanity that he witnessed in the Second World War and the woundedness of Christianity that he experienced growing up, convinced him of the necessity to work to restore the Church to its full health, to heal the wounds.

What is the theology behind ecumenism?

One might well wonder why there is this sudden enthusiasm for Christian unity. For many years, some would say, the various denominations have gone about their business, sometimes in an atmosphere of bitter sectarianism, at other times more or less peacefully. In either case Christians seemed to have accepted the status quo in a spirit of resignation as if nothing could be done about it. Why this change in attitude now? These questions are important; in fact they are fundamental to understanding ecumenism today. Without satisfactory answers no sustained commitment to ecumenism is possible.

"You forget dears . . . not only is it Reverend Mother's Day . . . it is also International Women's Year!!"

"I can't help feeling that when we said 'I believe', we all did, and now I say 'we believe', we all believe something different!"

Let us attempt to outline the thinking that can encourage a change of heart and sustain commitment and then describe some aspects of ecumenical theology. Let me stress in passing that the intellectual side is not enough by itself; it needs prayer and engagement in ecumenical activities as well. Ecumenism engages the mind, heart and will. All these elements are essential. We shall be returning to this point in more detail later on.

It has to be stated that the basis of this movement to restore the lost unity of Christianity is firstly theological. We can anchor it scripturally in the verse from John's gospel, Chapter 17, which refers to the prayer for unity: "May they all be one. Father, may they be one in us, as you are in me and I am in you" (17: 21). This is taken by Christians to show the will of Christ that his followers be one, not divided into a multiplicity of factions. It is not simply the will of a preacher, or archbishop, or moderator; it is the will of Christ, the founder of Christianity. As such it should carry the full weight of his authority and be taken very seriously by all Christians. It is not an optional extra. Christ willed his followers to be one and as this is clearly not the case now, Christians are committed to restore this lost unity which Christ willed for his Church. The mission of the Church, which is to carry on the work of Christ on earth, must thus include working towards this end.

In addition to this, the Church has the obligation to give witness to what Christ taught and preached. Unity was one of these. Therefore the life of the Church must give visible witness to Christian unity. Insofar as it does not, it is not sufficiently "Church". Some churches have traditionally given much emphasis to "giving witness", often in the context of giving witness to the working of grace in their lives, through conversion experiences or the like. Giving witness to unity today means that Christians must convincingly show the world that they have taken the issue seriously and are actively doing something to restore unity.

Having identified the foundation for ecumenism in Christ's will for unity and having stated that the Church must give witness to this unity, let us now try to describe the characteristics of an ecumenical theology. What does it look like? What are some of its features? In posing these questions we are not saying that ecumenical theology is some esoteric, new theology that someone has concocted. It should rather be seen as a perspective on all theology. Some aspects are as old as the Christian tradition itself, other aspects refer rather to the method of doing theology, which is becoming increasingly important in our world.

Ecumenism is firstly characterised by a search for truth, trite as that may sound. This search can be done individually, but is even more valuable when done with other churches as is the case in the official and unofficial dialogues. All churches have to be honest with themselves and face up to the fact that they might not have the full truth in some things. Where this is the case, they must be prepared to change. Striving for unity requires, therefore, an openness to change which in turn means dying and being reborn, at least in some things. Both processes are painful, but by way of consolation, it is useful to recall that this is at the heart of Christianity—dying and being reborn in many different ways. Life is not about maintaining the status quo, it never has been. At its deepest level it is about dying and being reborn in small and in big ways. The ultimate specification of this mystery, theologically speaking, is in the Paschal Mystery which was all about dying and being reborn in the resurrection to new life.

A second and fundamental dimension to appreciate is that ecumenical theology is a theology of sources and origins. Ecumenism goes back to the origins of Christianity. It looks at the original inspiration in the life of Christ and asks if we are being faithful to that charter. It looks at the Scriptures, the Fathers and early Church history to see where we have come from and whether our current direction is in continuity or discontinuity with that past. This explains why the statements that come from dialogues are so heavily scriptural and grounded in the early Church traditions.

Thirdly, it is a theology of fellowship, *koinonia*, which is the present preferred way of thinking of Church, which finds a resonance in the hearts of many believers. There are different ways of seeing the Church and each has its own validity. The Church is a multifaceted reality and its richness is not exhausted by the many images we have of it. Some images appeal more than others to Christians at given eras in the Church's history. In Roman Catholicism, between Vatican I (1870) and the election of Pope John XXIII (1958), the image of the Church as an hierarchical institution had very strong appeal. Currently among many Christian churches, the favoured image seems to be that of the Church as *koinonia*. (This is not to deny that the Church is also a hierarchically structured institution.)

What is meant by this term *koinonia*? Is it yet another churchy word to confound and mystify the average person? I would hope not. The Greek word *koinonia* comes from *koinos*, meaning "common, sharing, holding in common". By it is meant that all Christians share something in common. And what is it they share?

Christians share many things. They might share a common primary school, lamington drives, church building or community hall with others, or they might share their interests in helping the poor or giving aid to Third World countries. All these things are examples of sharing and we know from our experience that sharing helps to bind people together. However, sharing allows of degrees. Obviously sharing a building with someone is a very superficial sharing, compared with, perhaps, working side by side on raising money for the poor. It can be even more profound than this. Let me give another example. A husband and wife share all of their lives in marriage. They live together under the same roof and share all life's good and bad times together. This is not the superficial sharing of a school working bee. One could say they share their life with their partner on a very intimate and personal level. Unfortunately, as we know, divorce today often cuts off this sharing of lives when marriage partners choose to have nothing more in common with each other.

We say that married people share their lives and this is true. There is another dimension to this which is more philosophical and that is that we all share life in the sense of existence. I have existence, my friend has existence, others live, that is, they exist. Insofar as they all have existence they share "life". We have this in common. And insofar as God exists we share this dimension with God.

However, what we want to say now goes even beyond these levels of sharing. We refer to the most profound sharing that Christians have—namely they share God's life with God, in the first instance at God's invitation through Jesus Christ. We call this grace, but it is basically a relationship of love with God whereby we are invited to share in his personal life at an intimate level. This is, if you like, the vertical dimension of *koinonia*—oneself and God. Other Christians also share God's life with God, so we have this aspect in common with them—this is the horizontal dimension of *koinonia*.

From here one can tease out this fundamental relationship in terms of other things we share with Christians. We seal our relationship with God through baptism—Christians have this in common. They share the promise of justification through faith and a glorious resurrection with other Christians. In short, they share a common spiritual heritage earned through the death and resurrection of Christ. All this they have in common, so we feel this can be expressed in the term *koinonia*.

Ecumenical theology is a theology which stresses this commonality among Christians. People today find this a forceful, compelling and profound way of viewing Church.

If we try to translate this word *koinonia* into English, we have some problems. Some use the word "communion" and see the Church as "communion". Although the Second Anglican-Roman Catholic International Commission (ARCIC II) has adopted this,[4] I feel that this is not very satisfactory because many, especially Roman Catholics and Anglicans, use that word for the reception of the consecrated bread and wine[5]. Talking about Church as "a community of believers" misses some dimensions of the richness of the meaning of *koinonia*, but at least it avoids the ambiguous term "communion". Other churches have used the term "fellowship" which to some ears might emphasise a spirit of camaraderie rather than point to the very profound meaning of *koinonia* mentioned above. Whatever term we choose to use, it needs to be re-defined to incorporate the richness and insights of the word *koinonia*.

We mentioned that ecumenical theology was a theology of sources and we have a good example here. The concept of *koinonia* is really an ancient one going back to the Old Testament. The story of creation tells us how human beings were created for communion with God and with each other and how this relationship was ruptured by sin and restored in the covenants made through Moses and Abraham. In the New Testament the communion is with God the Father, through his Son in the Spirit, and with each other. This constitutes the people of the New Covenant.

At this point the relevance of the above to ecumenism can be clearly seen, because this communion which is the Church, entails the existence of a Church as a visible sign. As a sign it both represents and actually embodies the communion of human beings with God and with one another. However, this sign is obscured by the sinfulness of its members and their divisions. The Church is also a sign in a slightly different sense. It is said to be a sign and instrument of salvation because it is through the community called Church that Christ offers salvation. In this sense the Church is a "sacrament". Disunity among Christians weakens the credibility and obscures the sign value of the Church. The history of Christian missionary activity throughout the world has provided the sad proof of this statement. Therefore, it is up to Christians today to realize this fact and to do something about it.

The aptness of the understanding of the Church as *koinonia* could be summarized as follows. It emphasises what we Christians have in common, our sharing of God's life and the fact that we are brothers and sisters in having this gift of salvation and this marvellous inheritance that makes us co-heirs with Christ. The profundity of what we share, of what we have in common, should put all else, including personal and historical squabbles, into perspective. This is the way an ecumenist sees it.

Fourthly, the theology of ecumenism is rooted and grounded in love, again a fairly conventional thing to say, but sometimes difficult to apply. What we are saying is that the overall motivation behind ecumenism must be Christian love and desire for unity. This emphasis on love is sorely tested on many occasions when Churches are misunderstood, or themselves give unintended offence to other Churches. Some of the reports from current dialogues, which we will mention later, show that Churches are still giving offence and causing tensions. Accusations of proselytism and persecutions are still being made today. In the light of this one has to remind oneself that if the motivation for ecumenism is anything less than it being Christ's will, such problems might be too great to overcome.

Dialogue and the art of listening

We can now move on to two points relating to the method of doing ecumenical theology. The theology of ecumenism, it is said, is also very much a theology of dialogue—a word that has almost been done to death through excessive use. It implies, nonetheless, that Christians must be prepared to take the trouble of getting to know each other so that they are able to discuss their commonalities and differences in a friendly atmosphere. Some of the recent history of these dialogues is taken up in later chapters of this book. The past was marked by a lack of communication and, as we know from our knowledge of interpersonal relationships, zero communication means the end of personal relationships.

With good communication comes the possibility of understanding what the other is actually saying, not what we want to hear, or what third parties have said about them. Genuine communication prevents us imposing our own predetermined mindset on what others say.

Listening, really listening to others, is an art. Thus we can also say that a theology of ecumenism is a theology of mutual understanding. One can develop this point further and say that understanding people is helped by understanding their story, their history. This being the case, ecumenism must always include the history of the origins of Churches from as unbiased a position as possible.

The theology of ecumenism is also a theology of discovery or re-discovery. As Christians talk and pray together they find out things about each other and their churches which have been hidden or obscured in the past, when differences were highlighted. So Christians have re-discovered that they are already united in some degree by their Christian baptism. It is not as if they start off having absolutely nothing in common. They have re-discovered the Scriptures and prayer together, the centrality of the eucharist and the importance of ministry. Many other things are coming into focus through conversations and dialogues, both formal and informal. Working towards discovering and sharing all these things obscured by past differences is what ecumenism is all about.

It is for this reason that a book such as this must necessarily recall, or at least refer to, some of that history. In the next chapter we will do just that by giving an overview of the origins of the ecumenical movement and some early attempts to heal the wounds.

* * *

Discussion questions

1. What have been your own encounters with ecumenism over the last five, ten or twenty years? What have been some of the attitudes to ecumenism you have come across?

2. Do you find the reasons for promoting ecumenism as presented here convincing? Why or why not?

3. How have you experienced Church? Why do you think people respond well to seeing Church as communion (*koinonia*)?

Notes

1. The statistics on which this chart is based are taken from D. Barrett (ed.), *World Christian Encyclopedia*, Nairobi & London, OUP, 1982, pp. 815–848. The figures used were projections for 1985 based on extensive

research over 12 years. Later statistics for some churches are available but it is difficult to obtain comparative figures for a given year for all churches. Barrett provides the best comparison. The rounded-off figures in millions are as follows: Roman Catholic: 872; Orthodox: 170; Protestant: 278.

2. *Pastor and Priest*, Australian Lutheran-Roman Catholic Dialogue, Adelaide, Lutheran Publishing House, 1990, p. 3.

3. Cf. R. Brico, *Taizé: Brother Roger and His Community*, London, Collins, 1978.

4. Cf. *Church as Communion: An Agreed Statement by the Second Anglican-Roman Catholic International Commission, ARCIC II*, London, Church House Publishing & Catholic Truth Society, 1991.

5. C. Hill also makes this point; for a more detailed history of the term *koinonia* cf. his book, *The Mystery of Life: A Theology of Church*, Melbourne, Collins Dove, 1990, pp. 22–39. Cf. also for *koinonia* the document of the Joint Working Group of the World Council of Churches and the Roman Catholic Church entitled, *The Church: Local and Universal*. Especially relevant is the section entitled, "The Ecclesiology of Communion", *One in Christ*, Vol. XXVII, No. 3, 1991, # 5–10, pp. 269–72. Cf. also the document, *Church as Koinonia: Gifts and Calling*, of the Seventh General Assembly of the WCC, Canberra, 1991.

CHAPTER TWO

A Short History
of Ecumenism

We can sometimes forget what Christianity is all about. I am thinking of the little old lady who went to church regularly. She was a Roman Catholic and had great difficulty with the changes introduced by Vatican II. In particular she disliked all the singing and movement in the modern liturgy. She refused to give the kiss of peace during the eucharistic celebration, because, as she said, "I come here to praise God, not to be nice to people"!

It is in exploring the history of ecumenism that one is brought sooner or later to the question of what Christianity is all about. Like the little old lady, we might have to revise our ideas! We will also see that, although one is inclined to think of ecumenism as a recent thing, in reality the attempts to bring divided Christians together is not new. In fact, it is as old as Christianity itself. But before we examine that, the more obvious question that people ask is: what is ecumenism? This is understandable as not everyone is familiar with the word "ecumenism", and, secondly, the word itself is not self-explanatory, unlike other words used in similar contexts such as those in the phrases "interfaith dialogue" or "interchurch meetings".

What is ecumenism?

The word *"ecumenism"* or its adjective, *"ecumenical"*, has changed its usage over the centuries. The Greek word οικουμενε (*oikoumene*) literally means "that which pertains to the whole inhabited world". Matthew uses it in this sense in 24:14, "This Good News of the Kingdom will be proclaimed to the whole world (*oikoumene*) as a witness to all the nations."[1] Initially it was used in this sense in the life of the Church. Thus the first few councils of the Christian Church, like Nicea (325), Constantinople (381), Ephesus (425), or Chalcedon (451) were called "Ecumenical Councils" as they were seen to represent the whole, universal Church. This usage of the word is still current as when Vatican II is referred to by Roman Catholics as an ecumenical council. (Some Greek Orthodox adherents would however say that Vatican II is not an ecumenical council because it did not involve the entire Christian Church—Orthodox and Protestants were only present as observers. Cf. Appendix E).

There is a second meaning of the word "ecumenical". *It means that which pertains to Christian unity.* Thus the "ecumenical movement"[2] is "the process towards a greater expression of unity and cooperation among all Christians."[3] Although it refers to *Christian* unity in the first place, by extension it is also sometimes used to apply to efforts towards greater understanding and cooperation between Christians and persons of other world religions, e.g., Hindus, Moslems, Buddhists or Jews. As this can be confusing, I think it is clearer to use the term "interfaith" when at least any two world faiths are involved. Thus one can have "interfaith dialogues", or "interfaith prayer meetings" such as the one John Paul II hosted in Assisi on 27 October 1986, to which international religious leaders came. There is another substantial difference between the (Christian) ecumenical movement and interfaith (world religions) dialogue. The first has Christian unity as its goal; the second aims at better understanding and toleration between world religions, not organic, or any other type of unity, which would be impossible because of radical differences in belief. When one speaks of interfaith dialogues, it is important to point out in passing that the Christian-Jewish relationship is a unique one because of the related histories of these two faiths.

When did ecumenism start?

It is often thought that ecumenism is something which only started this century. This is not strictly speaking correct. Although it is correct to speak about the recent ecumenical movement as beginning at the 1910 Edinburgh Missionary Conference there were other attempts at Christian unity.

Already in New Testament times disunity created problems. We know from our reading of the letters, there were tensions and divisions among some of the communities. Paul has to make a strong exhortation to unity in belief and practices in 1 Corinthians 1:10–16 because there were factions within the community pulling it in different directions, some supporting Paul, others Cephas or Apollos. In Ephesians 4:1–6, allusion is made to the same sort of problem. In another local church, the Philippian community, two women, Evodia and Syntyche, were at loggerheads, so Paul called on them to make up and asks Syzygus, perhaps a community leader, to play the role of facilitator in the reconciliation (Philippians 4:2–3). One could find other examples of divisions and tensions in the New Testament communities, but the point has been made that divisions and attempts at reconciliation are there in our religious history right from the beginning.

In other early Church writings, we also find mention of disunity. Clement I, in his letter to the Corinthians (#46), calls on them to show unity. He found himself in a predicament when some members tried to throw out the local clergy! He had to remind them that the presbyters had been duly appointed and could not be dismissed by the parishioners.

Ignatius, the bishop of Antioch, writing in the early second century, had to contend with many heresies such as Docetism and Gnosticism and the influence of the Judaizing Christians. Not surprisingly, the theme of unity is never far from his thoughts. He exhorts the Magnesians to be submissive to their bishop (he makes the point frequently!) and to one another, as the Apostles were to Christ and the Father, "so that there may be complete unity in the flesh as well as in the spirit". So central was unity to Ignatius' thinking that, when writing to a fellow bishop, Polycarp, he forthrightly advises: "Give thought especially to unity, for there is nothing more important than this".

In another letter, Ignatius encourages the Philadelphians to avoid "all disunion and misguided teaching", to "cherish unity and shun divisions", and promises that those who have rejected their bishop may come back "into the unity of the Church and with God" if they repent. "Where disunion and bad blood exist", he points out, "God can never be dwelling". In a similar vein, he repeats this message to the Smyrnaeans: "Abjure all factions, for they are the beginning of evils". He also counsels them to work closely with their local bishop.

In the second and third centuries, there were many heresies, including Gnosticism, the secret knowledge of spiritual things, and Donatism.

Ironically the Donatists took the hardline regarding those who had rejected Christianity under pressure from paganism and then wanted to return to the fold. During this period we see the significant role that burgeoning heresies inadvertently played in the formulation of a definitive, orthodox creed. When heresies were abundant, everyone wanted to know who was right and who was wrong. Overseers, or bishops, had to spell out what the orthodox teaching was. Irenaeus found the problem so bad that he took up his pen to address the matter in his book, *Against Heresies.*

In medieval times one thinks of the Cathari, Waldensians, Albigensians, Hussites and others who were declared heretical and whose breakaway movements provided the occasion for the reconciliatory work of the Dominicans and Franciscans. However this was reconciliation by way of conversion and returning to the fold.

Here it might be useful to make the technical distinction between incorrect teaching, called 'heresy', and 'schism', which is a rupture of charity. The East-West Schism (which we will discuss in Chapter Three) was a schism but not a heresy. On the other hand, at the time of the sixteenth century Reformation, there were obvious differences in doctrine as well as failures in charity. The healing process in the case of a schism poses no doctrinal problems, but where heresy is alleged, the reconciliation process might be doctrinally lengthy and difficult. The implications of this distinction for the ecumenical process are obvious.

One of the most striking and bizarre episodes in the forgotten history of attempted reconciliations in Christianity was the attempt to heal the East-West Schism of 1054 by the Councils of Lyons (1274) and Florence (1439).

Some comment on these incidents is worthwhile because of the insights they provide. The Council of Lyons of 1274 was, in fact, the second council held in that French city. Called by Gregory X, it had as its agenda the Reform of the Church, union with the Greeks, and aid for the Holy Land. For political and financial reasons, the Emperor and the Pope were both keen on a reconciliation which was arranged prior to the actual Council. As Jedin says, "The union with the Greeks was realized because the Emperor had already previously declared for it in principle".[4] At the Council, the Emperor, Michael Paleologos, accepted the *filioque* clause (which we will come to in the next chapter—but briefly, it means changing the Creed to read, ". . . I believe in The Holy Spirit who proceeds from the Father *and the Son* . . .") as was reflected in their common profession of faith at the end of the Council.

Tragically, however, the reconciliation did not last long. The Byzantine clergy and people refused to accept what they saw as a capitulation. Johnson provides a graphic description of the Emperor's reaction to the opposition:

> The Emperor savagely tried to enforce compliance with his surrender. The public orator was flogged and exiled. One leading theologian was ordered to be scoured daily by his own brother until he submitted. Four of the Emperor's relatives were imprisoned and blinded; another died in prison; monks had their tongues torn out... All was in vain; when Michael died he was buried as a heretic in unconsecrated ground, and orthodoxy was restored in 1283, when *filioque* was again repudiated.[5]

The other bizarre incident was the attempt made at the Council of Ferrara-Florence to heal the East-West rift. The Council started off in Ferrara in 1438 with the Greek representatives arriving some months late. As in the earlier incident, both the Pope and the Emperor needed the reconciliation. The Patriarch of Constantinople at the time, Joseph II, was in favour of reunion but he died before the publication of the union decree in Florence. (The Council moved to Florence in January 1439 because of disease.)

At the Ferrara-Florence Council the points of contention between the Western Church and the Greeks were: the *filioque* clause, purgatory, the matter and form of the eucharist, and the interpretation of papal primacy. After much debate, an agreement entitled "*Laetentur coeli*", was in fact promulgated on 6 July 1439 and published in both Latin and Greek, with the Greeks once again accepting *filioque*. Sadly, as was the case with the Council of Lyons, the reconciliation did not last. "Soon after the Greeks left, and on the very return voyage, many of those among them who had taken part in the Council withdrew their consent".[6] The union was scarcely acknowledged in the East, even though other smaller groups of Oriental Christians—such as the Armenians, Copts, Syrians, Chaldees and Maronites—reached an understanding with the Western Church.

What history shows is that there have been many divisions among Christians since the very beginning, and equally that there have been many and various attempts at patching up differences. There has been the constant tension within Christianity created by the forces that work for unity and those that tend to destroy unity. After the split between Rome and Canterbury, Paul III made a last minute attempt at reconciliation with Henry VIII. He did this through his emissary, Guron

Bertano, in 1546, just prior to the Council of Trent. Henry however rejected the approach out of hand. Thereafter fewer and fewer efforts were made at reconciliation as the Christian denominations became entrenched in their prejudices. The Inquisition and its spiritual off-spring, spiteful sectarianism, left no room for healing.

Much later, in the nineteenth century, the formation of the various evangelical alliances witnessed to the strong ecumenical thrust in some parts of Christianity. One thinks of the London Missionary Society formed in 1795, and the Evangelical Alliance which came into being, also in London, in 1846.

Within some religious organizations there was the move to come closer together by way of setting up worldwide infrastructures. Thus the Lambeth Conference was constituted (1867), as was the World Alliance of Reformed Churches (WARC, 1875; now 180 member churches in over 80 countries), the World Methodist Council (1891) and the Baptist World Alliance (1905). Lutheran Churches were loosely affiliated in 1923 through the Lutheran World Convention which developed into the Lutheran World Federation (1947) and today represents 106 member churches. Founded in 1844, the Young Men's Christian Association (YMCA) provided for ecumenical coop-eration in particular projects. There are also regional infrastuctures like the Middle East Council of Churches (MECC), the All Africa Council of Churches (AACC), and numerous national council of churches as we shall see below.

There were also other worthwhile ecumenical initiatives. During the period 1921 to 1926, the Malines Conversations between Roman Catholics and Anglicans were held, and in the United States of America, Fr Paul (Lewis T. Watson) of the Society of the Atonement introduced the Week of Prayer for Christian Unity. Originally this week was the idea of Abbé Paul Couturier of Lyons. In 1937 the same Abbé Couturier founded the Dombes Group—pastors and priests who met each year at the Trappist monastery of Dombes, France, for a kind of ecumenical retreat at which they got to know each other.[7]

As regards actual church unions, much has happened this century. There has been good news from all parts of the world. In Canada in 1925 the Methodist, Congregational and nearly half the Presbyterian Churches formed the United Church of Canada. In 1965 the Anglicans and the United Church (later to be joined by the Disciples of Christ) accepted common principles of union. In 1973 they produced a *Plan of Union.*

In the United Kingdom, the United Reformed Church (URC) came into being in 1972 with the union of the Presbyterian and Congregational Churches in England. In 1981 they were joined by the Churches of Christ which is a remarkable and unique union because this new church now combines infant and believers' baptism in the one union. Since then there have been many bilateral dialogues including the Roman Catholics, Church of England, Methodist, Church of Wales and Church of Scotland.

Since the 1950s there have been calls for union between four main Protestant churches in France: the Reformed Church, the Reformed Church of Alsace and Lorraine, the Church of the Augsburg Confession of Alsace and Lorraine, and the Lutheran Evangelical Church. At the 1960 RCF (Reformed Church in France) assembly at Montbeliard, a vote for unity was carried, and at Colmar in 1966 a common profession of faith was drafted. There was a further call for unity in 1991 at the annual synod of the Reformed Churches in Orthez.

One sometimes forgets that there are Protestants in Italy. Not only have some of them united but they have done so in an unusual manner. The Methodists and the Italian Reformed (Waldensians) "integrated" in 1979 while still retaining their individual church names. They share a common synod and in 1990 they showed their desire to cooperate more closely with the Baptists by forming a common synod with them.

In India in 1947 the Church of South India came into existence with the merger of the Anglican, Methodist and Presbyterian churches. Thirty years later, in 1977, this church united with five Lutheran churches to form the Church of Christ in South India. In the same year the Church of North India was formed by the union of Anglicans, Presbyterians, Congregationalists, Baptists, Brethren, Disciples and Methodists.

In Australia there was also an encouraging sign of vitality in the ecumenical field with the formation of the Uniting Church of Australia in 1977. Here the partners were the Methodist, Congregational and some of the Presbyterian churches. In Uruguay, South America, the Christ Church was the result of the Emmanuel Methodist Church and the Holy Trinity Anglican Church merging in 1977. In 1981, in what was then East Germany (the Communist Democratic Republic of Germany), the Federation of Protestant Churches, the United Lutheran Evangelical Church and the Evangelical Church formed the United Protestant Church.

The ecumenical spirit was felt even in Japan with its minute Christian population. In 1982 the United Church of Christ in Japan (the Kyodan) and the Korean Christian Church in Japan covenanted to cooperate in certain areas.

Normally the churches that have united can be spotted by their name—it usually has the word "united" somewhere in the title, such as in the United Reformed Churches (URC) in England and Wales, or the United Church of Canada (UCC), or the United Methodist Church (USA). "United" implies some kind of agreement already achieved. However, others prefer to indicate that although some degree of union has been achieved, the process is as yet incomplete. Further steps of union need to be taken. Such, for example, is the case with the "Uniting" Church of Australia, the title of which subtly indicates that union is a continuing process. Still others give no indication in their titles that any unions have taken place, for example, the Church of Christ in South India or Christ Church (Uruguay).

In addition to all these positive steps, one should remember that many countries now have national church bodies actively facilitating the process of bringing the churches together. In the USA they are the National Council of Churches (NCC) and the Consultation on (US) Church Union (COCU)[8], in Britain it is the Council of Churches for Britain and Ireland, in Australia the Australian Council of Churches, in Canada the Canadian Council of Churches, etc. In New Zealand, the National Council of Churches died a natural death in 1987, only to rise again in a transformed body called the Conference of Churches in Aotearoa/New Zealand (CCANZ).

The Roman Catholic Church is unfortunately often not a member of these national councils, but things are changing. The British Council changed its constitution and name to form a new body which includes the Roman Catholics. The Australians are in the process of doing the same, and the NCC would like to follow. So there is plenty of evidence of ecumenical goodwill among these bodies.

Not to paint too rosy a picture, it should be remembered that there are failures in bringing churches together too. One notable one was the attempted covenant in the United Kingdom of the Anglicans, Methodists, Moravians and United Reformed Churches in the early 1980s. After years of negotiations it was abandoned. Other attempts at union or cooperation seem to drag on endlessly, e.g., the question of Roman Catholic membership of some national bodies such as the NCC (USA), or of the World Council of Churches.

Other than the tendency in recent times to bring churches together in union, there has also been the opposite movement. When some members disagree strongly with decisions in their church, they sometimes break away and form splinter churches. They do this either because their church is too conservative or too progressive. In the USA a small group of moderates who did not like the fundamentalist approach of the Southern Baptist Convention (the second largest Christian church in the USA after the Roman Catholic Church), formed their own Cooperative Baptist Fellowship (CBF). In Australia, Anglicans who do not support the ordination of women or divorce have formed the Anglican Catholic Church. And last century those who did not agree with Vatican I and the doctrine of Papal Infallibility formed the Old Catholics.

Unfortunately there are many examples of this tendency to fragmentation, although they tend to involve small numbers. Notwithstanding this fact the modern shift is unmistakably towards church unions.

The World Council of Churches

Much of the focus of ecumenism in the twentieth century has been rightly on the World Council of Churches, since it was the Protestants who took the initiative in matters ecumenical in recent times. The peak of the World Council of Churches lies in its General Assembly, the most recent of which was the Seventh Assembly, held in Canberra, Australia, in 1991. This meeting of the churches was all the more unforgettable because it was held against the backdrop of the Gulf War.

But let us examine the origins of the Council. Most writers would place the beginnings of the World Council of Churches with the Edinburgh World Missionary Conference of 1910. This conference was organized on an interdenominational basis which included Anglicans although they are not strictly speaking "Protestants".[9] The theme of the conference was that of the mission of the Church, as one would expect from the background of those who attended. This conference, which later became known as the International Missionary Council (IMC), eventually joined the World Council of Churches in 1961.

The International Missionary Council also encouraged the setting up of national missionary councils in other parts of the world whenever it had the opportunity. After Edinburgh, the International Missionary

Council met in Jerusalem (1928), then Madras, India (1938), and after the Second World War, at Whitby, England (1947), Willingen, Germany (1952), and Accra, Ghana (1957). At this latter meeting, it was proposed that it merge with the World Council of Churches which was done in 1961 at New Delhi.

Matters of doctrine and church order were deliberately avoided by the 1910 conference as the delegates wanted to concentrate on mission. However, one of the delegates, Bishop Brent, was planning to follow up the question of doctrine in another way later on, as he felt that matters of doctrine could not be avoided. This became the "Faith and Order" conference to which we will return below.

Meanwhile another movement was started in 1925, by the Archbishop of Uppsala, Nathan Söderblom (1865–1931), called the Life and Work Movement. Before we say more about the movement it will be useful to say something about the man.

Nathan Söderblom's father was a clergyman, so he grew up in a Swedish parsonage. His religious upbringing took place in an environment of profound evangelical piety and missionary interest. Not surprisingly, he followed in his father's footsteps and became a pastor in his church. Two important dimensions of his worldview are worth mentioning here: he was ecumenical and European in vision. The first of these two aspects was strongly influenced by his membership in the Student Christian Movement as a young man; the second by his experience as a pastor in Paris and subsequently as a professor in Germany. In addition to this, he had a strong conviction that Christian social movements had great potential for uniting Protestant churches.

Some thought he was a bit of a dreamer, and, given his particular religious upbringing, too much inclined to underestimate doctrinal and ecclesiastical differences. On the other hand, his many years of intense study in the history of world religions gave him a global perspective and a broad context for understanding the Christian faith, which compensated for any narrowness in his earlier religious education.

He was elected Archbishop of Uppsala in May 1914 after the outbreak of World War I. He immediately appealed for peace and Christian fellowship, but in vain. He initiated many peace proposals during the Great War which, although not fruitful, never discouraged him in his pursuit of peace—he was holding onto his vision. Eventually, as chairman of the Geneva Conference (1920), he was able to oversee the decision which called the Universal Conference of Life and Work into existence. It met in Stockholm in 1925, when Söderblom was 60 years old.

This Life and Work Movement, which Söderblom helped begin, was the second tributary of the river that eventually became known as the World Council of Churches. It was meant to be the practical face of Christianity, especially in the tragic aftermath of the First World War. The practical intent of those concerned was reflected in the topics they wished to see discussed at their first meeting. This was not going to be a pie in the sky conference, but a very relevant one, examining the Church and its attitude to economic, industrial, and international problems. Its practical orientation was captured by its slogan, "doctrine divides, service unites!".

In 1925, some 600 delegates, plus representatives of orthodox churches, met in Stockholm to discuss "The Church's responsibility for the total life of mankind"—a weighty topic! The opening sermon talked about setting up the kingdom of God in this complicated civilization of the twentieth century. This thrust was countered by a German bishop who objected: "Nothing could be more mistaken or more disastrous than to suppose that we mortal men have to build up God's kingdom in this world".[10] This tension between human and divine action, between the here-and-now and the eternal, immanence and transcendence, was to remain with this movement as unavoidable.

They met again at Oxford in 1937, just prior to the Second World War. The German delegates were forbidden by the state to attend. The clouds of conflict were once again gathering ominously. The theme this time was "Church, community and State", with the emphasis on letting the Church be Church. One delegate expressed it this way: "Our endeavour must be rooted in the whole doctrinal, educational and sacramental life of the Church." Although this represented a certain narrowing of vision in comparison to the global vision of the 1925 conference, the churches had nevertheless shown that they could grow closer while thinking together about the world's problems. This is still the case today—churches seemingly find it easy to work together on social issues, such as poverty, homelessness, the environment and disarmament.

The third tributary in this story is the Faith and Order Movement, mentioned above, which met for the first time in Lausanne, Switzerland, in 1927. As we saw, Bishop Brent (1862–1929) was one of the leaders at the Edinburgh World Missionary Conference in 1910 who was keen to examine doctrinal issues as well as practical ones.

Charles Brent was Canadian by birth. Ordained in 1886 in the diocese of Toronto, he moved to the United States of America and became an American citizen, settling in Boston. He was then made bishop and took the Episcopal Mission to the Philippines in 1902. By 1918 he was back in the United States and bishop of the Western New York Episcopalian Church. He was a chaplain in France during World War I. Thus like Söderblom, he lived through an era that shocked the world, and especially Europe, with its senseless killings. After the war he became an active member of the Faith and Order Movement, and was regarded as an international figure, being also president of the International Opium Commission.

In 1920 he was made chairman of the meeting in Geneva preparatory to the Lausanne Conference in 1927. As mentioned above, Bishop Brent had been keen on starting something in the area of doctrine and church order after Edinburgh. After canvassing support in Europe and a cold reception from Pope Benedict XV, the first World Conference of Faith and Order got underway in Lausanne in 1927 with Bishop Brent in the chair. Although the many and deep differences between denominations became clear at this conference, they nevertheless managed to produce one report that all could sign.

A second conference was held in Edinburgh in 1937, which agreed on a report on the meaning of the phrase "the Grace of our Lord Jesus Christ". There were many differences on the subjects of ministry and sacraments. (Not surprising given that it was only years later, in 1982, that the World Council of Churches produced its document on *Baptism, Eucharist and Ministry!*)

At this conference a vote was successfully taken to merge with the Life and Work Movement to form a World Council of Churches, but some voted against it fearing that it was "largely influenced by the passion for identifying Christianity with Socialism" and partly out of fear that a World Council of Churches would become a super-church (something that had to be expressly rejected at Toronto in 1952).

A year later at Utrecht, Holland, a provisional committee of the World Council of Churches was set up with William Temple as first chairman and Willem Visser 't Hooft as secretary. The first meeting was planned for August 1941, but because of the outbreak of World War II, it only eventuated in 1948. Temple in the meantime had died in 1944.

The background of the establishment of the World Council of Churches is thus one of unrest and war in Europe. On two occasions, in 1914–18 and 1939–45, the world had been at war with devastating results. After the First World War, the world watched only to see Germany, straining under the heavy penalties of the Versailles treaty, arm again under Hitler and march into Poland. Millions of people had lost their lives in the open trenches of the First World War and six million Jews had been massacred in the Holocaust of the Second World War. Cities and civilians had been obliterated. The first half of the twentieth century had been dominated by the wars. Everyone was sick of war, despair was everywhere, and people of goodwill looked for a future in which to hope. The coming together of the churches was in some way a symbolic phoenix amid the ashes and negativity of two world wars.

Against this background, the World Council of Churches was officially constituted in Amsterdam in 1948. Its constitution states:

> The World Council of Churches is a fellowship of churches which confess the Lord Jesus as God and Saviour according to the Scriptures and therefore seek to fulfil their common calling to the glory of the one God, Father, Son and Holy Spirit.

The functions of the Council are clearly stated in its constitution. These have been refined over the years and today give sharper focus to the call for visible unity. The functions are:

1. to call the churches to the goal of visible unity in one faith and in one eucharistic fellowship expressed in worship and in common life in Christ;
2. to facilitate the common witness of the churches in each place and in all places;
3. to support the churches in their worldwide missionary and evangelistic task;
4. to express the common concern of the churches in the service of human need, the breaking down of barriers between people, and the promotion of one human family in justice and peace;
5. to foster the renewal of the churches in unity, worship, mission and service;
6. to establish and maintain relations with national councils and regional conferences of churches, world confessional bodies and other ecumenical organizations;
7. to carry on the work of the world movements for Faith and Order and Life and Work and of the International Missionary Council and the World Council on Christian Education.[11]

Who are its members?

The test of church membership, other than the profession of faith as mentioned above, is further carried out according to size and stability. A church with between 10,000 and 25,000 members can acquire associate membership status. With more than the latter figure it can become a full member. The first Assembly met in Amsterdam with a membership of 147 churches. Since then some churches have felt compelled to withdraw for a variety of reasons. The Chinese churches withdrew at the time of the Korean War. The Baptist churches of Scotland and the Netherlands have also withdrawn; the latter because of the imperialism of the national churches, rapprochement with Rome, the danger of Marxist infiltration, and a theology of relativism (some of these objections are still heard today!). The three Dutch Reformed Churches of South Africa originally withdrew in 1961 after the Cottesloe Consultation which condemned the theory and practice of apartheid.

Membership represents a great cross-section of religious traditions. One can cite almost the whole spectrum of Christian churches: Old Catholic[12], Eastern Orthodox, Oriental Orthodox, Baptist, Lutheran, Methodist, Anglican, United, Disciples, Brethren, Independent (Lord Aladura, Assyrian, African Israel Nineveh, African Holy Spirit, Hussite, Kimbanguist, Mar Thoma, Philippine), Reformed (including also Waldensian, Remonstant, Presbyterian, Mission Covenant, and Congregational), Moravian, Pentecostal, Quaker, and Mennonite. Evangelicals are found in many of these traditions.

There are of course, some noticeable absentees from the above list. Roman Catholicism, Adventism and the Salvation Army are outside World Council of Churches membership although they cooperate in other ways. Nevertheless total membership today is an impressive 320, giving some external expression to the desire for one faith and, indeed, for one world.

Structure of the World Council of Churches

Although organizational structures are often seen as the boring part of learning about institutions or systems, it is nevertheless important insofar as structures influence decisions. It follows that if one wishes to change a structure one must first understand how it operates.

The General Assembly is the large, governing body meeting about every 7 or 8 years. Since Amsterdam it has met in a variety of industrialized and developing countries from both the North and South:

1954: Evanston, USA

1961: New Delhi, India

1968: Uppsala, Sweden

1975: Nairobi, Kenya

1983: Vancouver, Canada

1991: Canberra, Australia

1998: ?

A central committee handles work in between General Assemblies. When the World Council of Churches was inaugurated, George Bell became the first chairman of the central committee, and Franklin Clark Fry vice-chairman. Fry, who was also president of the United Lutheran Church in America, later took over as chairman of the central committee until just before the Uppsala Assembly. In 1938, Willem Visser 't Hooft, who was a young 37-year-old Dutch minister at the time, became the first general secretary and remained in the job until 1966 (he died in 1985). Eugene Blake (1966–72), an American Presbyterian, followed, then the West Indian, Philip Potter (1972–84), and the South American, Emilio Castro (1984–92).

The World Council of Churches is basically funded by the subscriptions of individual members. Some large donations have helped, such as the J. D. Rockefeller Foundation which has financed the setting up of the Ecumenical Institute of the Chateau de Bossey in Switzerland, a few kilometres from Geneva. In 1990 over 70% of the funding came from Germany, Sweden and the United States of America.

Further structural detail of the World Council of Churches can be seen by referring to the chart on page 29. Mention was made above of a central committee. Currently this committee consists of 158 members and meets every 12 to 18 months. It has a 26-member executive committee which meets twice a year under the Secretary General, Emilio Castro. A Geneva staff of 270 sees to the daily running of business. There are basically four program units in which one can find the descendants of the earlier Faith and Order, Life and Work, and International Missionary conferences:

> Unity and Renewal;
>
> Mission, Education and Witness;
>
> Justice, Peace and Creation;
>
> Sharing and Service.

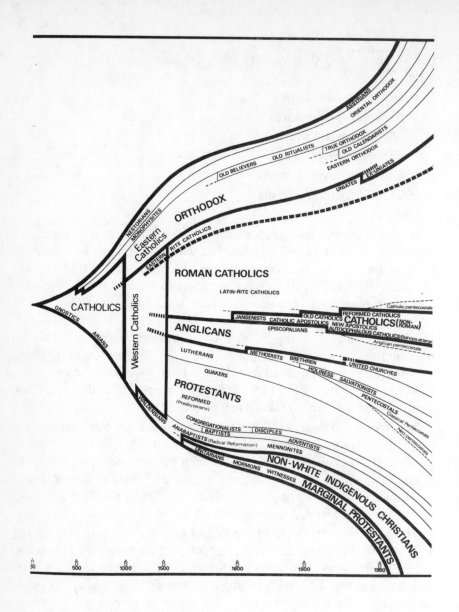

ORTHODOX

ASSYRIANS
ORIENTAL ORTHODOX
TRUE ORTHODOX
OLD CALENDARISTS
OLD BELIEVERS   OLD RITUALISTS   EASTERN ORTHODOX
EX-UNIATES
UNIATES

NESTORIANS
MONOPHYSITES
Eastern Catholics
EASTERN RITE CATHOLICS

ROMAN CATHOLICS

LATIN-RITE CATHOLICS

GNOSTICS   CATHOLICS

ARIANS

Western Catholics

Catholic pentecostals
REFORMED CATHOLICS
JANSENISTS   CATHOLIC APOSTOLICS   OLD CATHOLICS   NEW APOSTOLICS   CATHOLICS (NON-ROMAN)
EPISCOPALIANS   AUTOCEPHALOUS CATHOLICS Bishops at large
Anglican pentecostals

ANGLICANS

LUTHERANS   METHODISTS   BRETHREN   UNITED CHURCHES

QUAKERS   HOLINESS   SALVATIONISTS

PROTESTANTS   PENTECOSTALS

REFORMED
(Presbyterians)   Classical Pentecostals

WALDENSIANS   CONGREGATIONALISTS   DISCIPLES
BAPTISTS   Neo-Pentecostals
ANABAPTISTS (Radical Reformation)   ADVENTISTS
MENNONITES

UNITARIANS   MORMONS   WITNESSES   NON-WHITE INDIGENOUS CHRISTIANS
MARGINAL PROTESTANTS

30   500   1000   1500   1800   1900   1980

Timeline of the origins of the main Christian Churches

Structure of the WCC

MEMBER CHURCHES

ASSEMBLY

CENTRAL COMMITTEE
EXECUTIVE COMMITTEE

GENERAL SECRETARIAT
Office of the General Secretary
Church and Ecumenical Relations
Interreligious Relations
Communication
Programme Coordination
Finance and Administration

UNIT 1 - UNITY AND RENEWAL
Ecclesial Unity: Faith and Order
Inclusive Community
Ecumenical Theological Education
Worship annd Spirituality

UNIT 2 - MISSION, EDUCATION AND WITNESS
Mission in Unity
Evangelism
Education for All God's People
Community and Justice
Health and Healing
Gospel and Culture
Theological Significance of Religions

UNIT 3 - JUSTICE, PEACE AND CREATION
JPIC - An Educational and Conciliar Process
Theology, Ethics and Creation
Development and Socio-economic Justice
Indigenous People and Land Rights
Ecumenical Action on Racism
Churches in Solidarity with Women
Youth: Solidarity and Action
International Affairs, Peace and Human Rights

UNIT 4 - SHARING AND SERVICE
Sharing Ecumenical Resources
Understanding Diakonia
Meeting Urgent Human Need:
Emergencies, Refugees
Advocacy and Action with the Poor
Equipping and Linking Churches in Service

MEMBER CHURCHES

There are many program activities ranging over a very wide spectrum and representing an enormous agenda: faith and order, mission and evangelism, interfaith dialogue, church and society, inter-church aid, anti-racism, medical issues, international affairs, development, renewal and congregational life, youth, women, theological education, and education. One of the better known services of the WCC is the Commission on Inter-Church Aid, Refugee and World Service (CICARWS) because it is often in the news headlines regarding aid to countries like Ethiopia.

The World Council of Churches is a council of *churches*, not individuals, so all decisions need to be implemented by the churches. Its authority is moral, not jurisdictional. "The fact must be recognized that the Assembly possesses no authority to speak on behalf of the churches. And in no manner can it claim ... to be the *Una Sancta*, such as is assumed in the Papal *ex cathedra* utterances", said the Amsterdam Assembly.

What does it hope to do then? Basically Assemblies, in pursuing the aims of their constitution mentioned above, bring the churches out of their isolation to enable them to meet each other, to discuss common problems and, where possible, to formulate common policies and take common action.

Some structural weaknesses

There are some built-in weaknesses however, associated with Assemblies. With the high turnover of delegates from one Assembly to the next, continuity of thought and action is difficult. Participants come to Assemblies determined to renew the Church and world before the final plenary session. Assemblies are normally about two weeks in duration. This is a very short time bearing in mind that a council like Vatican II was a process that spread over three years.

There are some other built-in weaknesses as well. Like any big organization (including governments!) it runs the risk of being out of touch with its members. In its early days at least, it was very much a western, European organization, or as someone humorously said, the religious equivalent of NATO. Another weakness, which is not unique to this body, is that some decisions or statements are seen as political, especially when they concern social justice issues, such as the liberation movements throughout the world or attempts to combat racism. In such cases the decisions or programs are said to be "communist inspired" or the organization itself is discredited as being infiltrated by communists. This can lead to the alienation of some members, but now that communism itself has been discredited by its own, some other scapegoat will have to be found! It should be added that criticism that the World Council of Churches was communist inspired has been well matched over the years by critics at the other end of the spectrum who see it as an agent of capitalism. There is thus reasonable ground to believe that it might be somewhere between these two extremes!

Other serious weaknesses were highlighted at the 1991 Assembly, held in Canberra. Among others, the Orthodox participants raised some concerns which deserve to be noted. The Orthodox raised eight concerns in all, and summarized below they serve to indicate the problems.[13] There was concern that:

1. the goal of the restoration of the unity of the Church was being eclipsed by the wider unity of humanity and creation, valid goals though they be;

2. there is an increasing departure from the theological basis of the Council, threatening to make it a forum for every opinion;

3. there is a departure from the biblically-based Christian understandings of such concepts as the Trinitarian God, salvation, the 'Good News' of the gospel itself, human beings created in the image and likeness of God, and the Church;

4. there is a broadening of aims in the direction of relations with other religions without sufficient definition of the theological criteria to be used in such dialogue;

5. there is a tendency to substitute a private spirit, the spirit of the world or other spirits for the Holy Spirit in some of the themes presented at the Assembly;

6. there is a misunderstanding on the part of some of the Orthodox's abstinence from eucharistic communion, which they see as the expression of unity not a means to achieve it;

7. there is concern over the quota system of decision-making which could weaken the possibility of an Orthodox witness in an otherwise Protestant international organization;

8. the very nature and identity of the Council seemed to be questioned, taking all these tendencies into consideration.

I am not suggesting that all these points raised by the Orthodox participants are equally valid, but they do highlight the need for the Council to work out a thorough theology on many issues including ecclesiology and Christian ethics, unless it is satisfied to be a forum for any and every opinion without having one of its own. In being too accommodating it has perhaps neglected building up its own theology.

What about the Roman Catholics?

Officially the Roman Catholic Church did not fit into the ecumenical story at all for some time. The Council of Trent came too late after Luther and the Swiss Reformers to have any real chance to staunch the wound that became the Reformation. Once the opportunity of restoring unity had been allowed to evaporate, Roman Catholic attitudes towards Protestants became very negative, defensive and sometimes arrogant, especially on the part of the official representatives of Roman Catholicism.

An example of negative attitudes in recent times is the 1896 Roman document called *Apostolicae Curae*, which declared Anglican Orders invalid and therefore Anglican communion services invalid. The reason was not on the grounds that the apostolic succession had been lost at the Reformation, but because the ordinal (the official text used) by which Orders were conferred was deficient in its theology of the ministry and sacraments. The Church of England, it was said, did not 'intend' to do in ordination what the Roman Catholic Church does. This incident has caused much tension between Anglicans and Roman Catholics and is once again on the ecumenical agenda for re-examination.

Although the general attitude of the Roman Catholic Church towards Protestants was negative from the Reformation to Vatican II, there were some positive moments this century prior to 1963 in Roman Catholic-Protestant relations, mainly on the part of enlightened individuals. One was at the time of the 1910 Edinburgh Missionary Conference mentioned above. Although no invitations were sent to Rome, Mgr Bonomelli, the bishop of Cremona, sent a letter to the executive applauding the idea of the conference and asserted the need for spreading Christianity as the universal religion. He acknowledged an existing unity "great enough to warrant continuing further discussion, tending to promote the union of all believers in Christ".[14] (This seems to foreshadow the later *Baptism, Eucharist and Ministry* document of 1982, which speaks of the existing unity among Christians through baptism.)

However, the negative attitude of the Roman Catholic Church towards Protestants outweighed any positive moments. It was basically a question of declining invitations to cooperate and thus missing golden opportunities of showing goodwill. In 1918 the Secretary of State, Cardinal Gasparri, decided against sending representatives to a peace conference in spite of an invitation to do so. Rome was also invited to the Lausanne conference of Faith and Order in 1927, but declined. The official report says that "the official refusal of the invitation was balanced by the personal friendliness and benevolence of the Pope." However the decree of the Holy Office (set up at the time of the Inquisition, now called the Congregation for the Doctrine of the Faith) dated 8 July 1927, forbade Roman Catholics to attend the conference.

Worse was to come. In 1928 Pius XI issued his encyclical *Mortalium Animos*, which marks the absolute nadir in Catholic-Protestant relationships this century. The document was on "fostering true religious union", the implication being that attempts to date (by Protestants) had got it all wrong. Pius XI condemned meetings and conferences of every kind where believers and unbelievers mix and were invited to join in the discussions. This, he said, presupposes the erroneous view that all religions are more or less good and praiseworthy, an attitude which leads to naturalism and atheism. (It seems here the Pope was confusing two kinds of meetings, Stockholm and Lausanne were attended by Christians only; other interfaith and interreligious conferences had delegates who belonged to faiths other than Christianity. It also suggests that the Pope, or his offsiders, did not inform himself fully and with sufficient care about the issues—just as Pope Leo did not read Luther's complaints with full attention.)

The Pope went on to say that attempts at reconciliation were subversive to the foundations of the Catholic faith. The Roman Catholic Church is the one true Church and cannot be treated as one among many. The Church can by no means take part in these meetings. He stressed the obligation to hold equally all dogmas defined by Rome (whereas the later teaching of Vatican II spoke about the hierarchy of truths). *Mortalium Animos* ended with a familiar return-to-Rome theology:

There is but one way in which the unity of Christians may be fostered, and that is by furthering the return to the one true Church of Christ of those who are separated from it; far from that one true Church they have in the past fallen away.[15]

Understandably there was considerable reaction to *Mortalium Animos*. Söderblom rejected the caricature of ecumenism as depicted by Pius XI. On the Roman Catholic side many publications appeared which basically dissented from the papal attitude and promoted a positive approach to ecumenism. For example, journals such as *Irenikon*,[16] *Vers l'Unité Chretienne* and *Unitas,* sprung up.

Books such as *Um Kirchliche Einheit* (On Church Unity, 1929), by Max Pribilla, and *Chrétiens désunis: Principes d'un 'oecumenisme' catholique* (*Divided Christians: Principles for a Catholic ecumenism,* 1937), by the now famous Dominican theologian, Yves Congar, appeared, showing quite different thinking about ecumenism from within the Roman Catholic Church. They were very progressive for those times, especially in the context of *Mortalium Animos.* Congar's book ended with the vision, "it is not impossible that a measure of Catholic participation may be given to some part of the work of the ecumenical movement." Congar, after falling into disfavour in the 1950s over the *Théologie Nouvelle* (literally, "New Theology"; it refers to the renewal of theology, especially in France in the 1940s and 50s), was to be resurrected as one of the leading theological lights of Vatican II, especially in the area of ecumenism.

Another encouraging factor was the establishing of the *Una Sancta* movement in Germany in 1938. This was a movement which aimed at reconciling Roman Catholics and Lutherans. First attempts were made in Berlin in 1918 with the foundation of the Protestant High Church movement. Then, in 1928, Metzer united Catholics and Lutherans in his *Una Sancta* Brotherhood. He was later executed by the Nazis. A journal with the name *Una Sancta* was launched in 1946 with the aims of arriving at a new appraisal of Luther; of renewing the liturgy; of encouraging a scriptural renaissance; and of promoting an increased participation by the Roman Catholic Church. In addition to this it should be noted that World War II in general brought Catholics and Protestants closer together in Germany.

There was some breakthrough in official circles in 1937 when four Catholic priests and a layman attended the Faith and Order Conference in Edinburgh as unofficial observers. In 1939, to a request for unofficial contact by Dr Temple of the World Council of Churches, the Roman Catholic Secretary of State said that there would be no obstacle to his confidentially consulting English Roman Catholic bishops and the Apostolic Delegate, or to the exchange of confidential information and opinion with Roman Catholic theologians! The spirit of secrecy and the feeling of doing something not quite proper still prevailed!

As we saw, 1948 was the big year for the birth of the World Council of Churches, but the official Roman Catholic position had not changed. The Holy See refused permission to any Roman Catholic to attend the conference. As might be anticipated the occasion was met in the Catholic Press with a range of responses from scorn to enthusiasm.

Any changes in attitude on the part of Roman Catholicism were slow and painful. As a follow-up, an instruction to local bishops, on 20 December 1949, entitled *Ecclesia Catholica*, acknowledged that discussions on matters of faith and morals between Roman Catholics and other Christians had taken place in the past and would continue to do so in the future. It set out conditions for such talks which sound rather quaint in today's ecumenical atmosphere: they must have official sanction; all communication in sacred rites was forbidden; Catholics and other Christians could meet as equals. What it said about praying together would elicit wry smiles today: "It is not discountenanced to open and close the meetings with a common recitation of the Lord's Prayer or some other prayer approved by the Catholic Church".[17] According to some, this document marks the turning point in Roman Catholic-Protestant relationships. A turning point which was soon to become a complete U-turn under John XXIII and Vatican II.

The U-turns of Vatican II

For Roman Catholics though, the watershed in ecumenism was the Vatican II *Decree on Ecumenism*, with its Latin title, *Unitatis Redintegratio*, which translates as 'the restoration of unity'. It was one of the public aims of the Council to promote Christian unity (the other being to update the Church), so this document, although consisting of only twenty-four fairly brief paragraphs, is important in the overall impact of the Council. Historically this has been the case as the document registered a number of significant about-turns in Roman Catholic attitudes, even if some people think that in the years since the Council and especially this decade (the 1990s), some of the steam has gone out of the ecumenical locomotive.

The rationale of any ecumenism is mentioned in the first two paragraphs. It runs like this: Christ prayed that his Church may be one and that unity has been shattered. Christians need therefore to work for the restoration of Christian unity in faithfulness to the manifest will of Christ. There is no choice for those who call themselves Christians. It is not optional like some Christian charitable work above the call of duty. It is not something for the very holy as opposed to the average sinner in the pews. Lack of appreciating this rationale might, however, have something to do with the importance or otherwise of Scripture in a Christian's "religion". Christ's prayer for unity is worth repeating here: "May they all be one. Father, may they be one in us, as you are in me and I am in you, so that the world may believe it was you who sent me." (John 17:21)

No "Catholic" ecumenism

Given the history of Roman Catholic attitudes towards ecumenism since the encyclical *Mortalium Animos* it is no wonder that the first draft of the decree had as its title for Chapter 1, "The Principles of Catholic Ecumenism". Catholics have been used to a Catholic Women's League, a Catholic Boys Scouts Troop, a Catholic Bushwalking Club, so why not a Catholic ecumenism? This century the Protestants have set the pace in ecumenism (so much for it being a Roman plot!), so when the time was ripe for Catholics to join in, they understandably thought that they would run a parallel movement. However, this approach was soon challenged. If the Holy Spirit has fostered the movement towards greater Christian unity, then it "belongs" neither to Roman Catholics nor Protestants. It belongs to the Holy Spirit. Hence the title was changed to "Catholic Principles of Ecumenism". This registered a U-turn in thinking.

How is "ecumenism" understood?

The meaning of the ecumenical movement is tackled early on in the *Decree on Ecumenism* with the definition, "those activities and enterprises which, according to various needs of the Church and opportune occasion, are started and organized for the fostering of unity among Christians" (#4). It further speaks about "spiritual ecumenism", by which it means promoting ecumenism through holiness of life and praying for unity, in other words, the kind of ecumenism that everyone can practise.

An important distinction is also made between ecumenical action and conversions to a particular Christian denomination. The process whereby someone might "convert" to another denomination is quite different to what we mean by ecumenical actions. In the history of dialogues and ecumenical happenings since this decree, this does not seem to have been a problem, although proselytism continues to be a burning issue in some parts of the world such as the Ukraine, Ethiopia, South America, the Philippines and the South Pacific Islands. We will return to this in Chapter Five.

Another big U-turn manifest in the document is the confession that no one was blameless in the many disputes over centuries that spawned so many splits in Christianity. Referring to these rifts, the document says that in these unfortunate developments people "of both sides were to blame". That admission of guilt is the beginning of a positive move forwards, since up to that moment the Roman Catholic Church had always seen itself as in the right and that others, being in the wrong, must repent and return to the fold. The traffic was one-way in a "return-to-Rome" theology. Now the decree, at least in parts, gives the impression of a pilgrim Church moving towards Christ.

Membership of the Church?

There is an ecclesiological problem in the document. Who are members of the Church? Those who believe and are baptized are brought into a certain, though imperfect union with the Catholic Church (#3). Are they therefore members of the Catholic Church? The *Baptism, Eucharist and Ministry* document[18] speaks about Christians, through baptism, being brought into union with Christ, with each other and with the Church of every time and place (#6). This Church is unspecified, but must be taken to mean the "Christian Church". Differences of doctrine or church order can be serious, says the decree, and be obstacles to full ecclesiastical communion. In other words, the Roman Catholic Church is still thinking of itself as the One, Holy, Catholic and Apostolic Church and the other Christian churches as being in union with it to a greater or lesser degree. Perhaps the image of concentric circles best illustrates this theology.

If one digresses for a moment and goes back to the Vatican II constitution on the Church, *Lumen Gentium*, the Roman Catholic point was that the Church of Christ "subsists in" the Catholic Church. It sees itself as the fullest embodiment of the Church Christ founded: "This Church, constituted and organized in the world as a society, subsists in the Catholic Church, which is governed by the successor of Peter and by the bishops in union with that successor, although many elements of sanctification and of truth can be found outside of her visible structure. These elements, however, as gifts properly belonging to the Church of Christ, possess an inner dynamism toward Catholic unity" (#8).

Some of these "elements" are specified in the decree as "the written word of God; the life of grace; faith, hope, and charity, along with other interior gifts of the Holy Spirit and visible elements" (#3). These provide access to salvation, the decree admits, which again is a U-turn from the much-publicized doctrine, *Extra Ecclesiam Nulla Salus* (No salvation outside the Church, meaning, the Roman Catholic Church). The Roman Catholic Church is said in the document to be "the all-embracing means of salvation".

On the doctrinal level two points are of interest. Firstly, the decree makes the distinction between the "deposit of Faith" (what an unfortunate expression!) and the formulation of doctrine (#6). This is a significant advance and encourages the proponents of the development of doctrine. Secondly, it speaks of a hierarchy of truths, which vary in their relationship to the foundations of the Christian faith (#11). These two together have helped to make dialogue with other Christian churches easier for Roman Catholics in recent times. On a practical level Christians should start with what unites them, as for centuries they have concentrated on what divided them. At the same time, what the document calls a false irenicism, a pretending that no problems exist, should be avoided. The slogan "doctrine divides, action unites" needs to be balanced with an emphasis on the importance of doctrine in a future re-united Church.

At the centre of the decree is the sentence that there will be no ecumenism without a change of heart (#7). All Christians need to examine their attitudes towards each other and their Christian faith. This could begin by avoiding in expression whatever might be offensive to members of other churches. For example, instead of defining people negatively as "non-Catholics" or "non-Protestants"(!), one could refer to them as "members of other Christian churches". Roman Catholics would not like to be referred to as Non-Protestants! Hopefully a new language would help people to think differently of each other, increase mutual respect, and open the way for serious dialogue.

On the question of power and jurisdiction we can note at least one statement. In speaking of its relationship with the Eastern Churches (a delicate ecumenical subject if ever there was one), the decree says that previous councils have proclaimed that in order to restore communion, one must "impose no burden beyond what is indispensable" (Acts

15:28; #18). This little quote will no doubt not be forgotten in future dialogues, since one of the complaints of Eastern Churches like the Ukrainian Church (which is within Roman Catholicism) is about the imposition of non-essentials on their rite by Rome. This has all sorts of ramifications for dialogues between Anglicans, Orthodox, Protestants and Roman Catholics in working through issues of church order and the role and jurisdictional powers of a pope or patriarch figure.

There is another important point arising from Vatican II which is worth highlighting. It is the restoration of Scripture in the life of the Roman Catholic Church to a central position. This would have to be one of the major lessons learnt from Protestantism. For a church that since the Reformation tended to focus more on the sacraments than on the Word, it is good to read this statement that draws a parallel between the eucharist and the Word: "Just as the life of the Church grows through persistent participation in the eucharistic mystery, so we may hope for a new surge of spiritual vitality from intensified veneration for God's word, which 'lasts forever'".[19]

This chapter has traced the history of ecumenism from earliest times to the era of cooperation between Christian churches. In passing I have mentioned the two[20] main rifts in Christianity, namely the East-West Schism and the Protestant Reformation. In the next chapter we will consider the first of the two rifts, the East-West Schism, and seek to understand some of the circumstances as these throw light on contemporary dialogues.

* * *

Discussion questions

1. What experience have you had of talking to people from other Christian churches about Christianity? What have you learnt from them?

2. How would you explain, in your own words, what "ecumenism" is all about to a friend who asked?

3. Do you know of any ecumenical events in your local area?

4. How would you describe the contribution of the World Council of Churches to ecumenism?

5. Refer to the eight concerns of the Orthodox participants regarding the trends within the World Council of Churches (page 31). How important and valid do you think they are?

Notes

1. It is used elsewhere in the New Testament with some slight differences in meaning, cf. Romans 10:18; Hebrews 1:6; Luke 2:1; Acts 17:6; 17:31; 19:27; Revelation 3:10.
2. The expression "ecumenical movement" was first used by A. Deissmann in an address concluding the Stockholm Conference in 1925. Cf. P. Meagher, et al., (eds), *Encyclopedic Dictionary of Religion*, Vol. A to E, Washington, Corpus Publications, 1979, p. 1157.
3. Ibid.
4. Cf. H. Jedin (ed), *History of the Church*, Vol. IV, London, Burns and Oates, 1980, p. 205.
5. Cf. P. Johnson, *A History of Christianity*, Harmondsworth, Penguin Books, 1976, p. 187.
6. Jedin, op. cit., p. 480.
7. Cf. J. Comby, *How to Read Church History*, London, SCM Press, 1989, p. 208.
8. It consists of nine member churches: African Methodist Episcopal, African Methodist Episcopal Zion, Christian Methodist Episcopal, (Anglican) Episcopal, United Methodist Churches, Christian Church (Disciples of Christ), International Council of Community Churches, Presbyterian Church (USA) and United Church of Christ.
9. The origin of the word "Protestant" was the occasion at the Diet of Speyer in 1529 when the minority of the princes favourable to the Reformation delivered a 'Protest' against the proceedings of the emperor Charles V and the Catholic princes. Cf. O. Chadwick, *The Reformation*, Harmondsworth, Penguin Books, 1968, p. 62.
10. B. Till, *The Churches Search for Unity*, Harmondsworth, Penguin Books, 1972, p. 200.
11. D. Gill, (ed), *Gathered for Life*, Geneva, WCC, 1983, pp. 324–5.
12. They were formed by three national Catholic splits, one in the Netherlands in the eighteenth century, the second in Austria-Hungary after Vatican I, and the third in the USA in the nineteenth century. The first two groups came together in 1889 through the Treaty of Utrecht. Worldwide they number about half a million.
13. Cf. *Ecumenical Press Service*, 11–25 March 1991, 91.03.49.
14. Cf. R. Rouse & S. Neill (eds), *A History of the Ecumenical Movement*, London, SPCK, 1953, p. 681.
15. Ibid., p. 683.
16. This quarterly journal was published by the monks of Amay-sur-Meuse, Belgium, to promote harmony with Eastern churches, which was the

reason the monastery was founded. Its liturgy was celebrated in the Latin and Byzantine rite.

17. Cf. Rouse & Neill, op. cit., p. 692.
18. World Council of Churches, *Baptism, Eucharist and Ministry*, Faith and Order Paper No. 111, Geneva, WCC, 1982, p. 3.
19. *Verbum Dei*, #26, in *The Documents of Vatican II*, ed. W. Abbott, London, Geoffrey Chapman, 1972.
20. Some commentators would say there have been three rifts, the first being the rift between the Jews and Christians in the first century.

CHAPTER THREE

The Churches
of the East

Recently I was invited to attend the Sunday service of a local Coptic church. Not knowing much about this Orthodox church I was keen to go and learn what I could through experiencing its liturgy. The priest said I could come at about nine o'clock, although they would be starting earlier. As I recall it, the congregation was chanting prayers when I arrived which I took to be the Divine Office, or the Coptic equivalent. The Sunday liturgy (eucharistic celebration) began sometime after that. Although I recognized the parts of the liturgy, they were very drawn out by my standards. Over and above this it happened to be the feast-day of their patron saint, Saint Bishoy, which meant a procession of icons and hymn singing around the interior of the church that appeared to go on endlessly. This took place, as I recall, just after the readings, which by the way, included a lengthy reading in Coptic from the life of Saint Bishoy.

When I finally had to leave, some two hours later, the liturgy had not yet reached the Rite of Communion! I was told the session actually started at eight in the morning and went on for about four hours. The length of time taken over the liturgy, the prayers in Coptic and Egyptian, the singing, the ancient rituals such as the celebrant examining at length various loaves of bread before selecting one for the altar while the choir chanted, the communal confession of sins at the beginning in separate rooms for men and women—all these combined to put me into a different time zone and a different religious world. I could not help comparing this experience with the no-frills Sunday liturgies with which I am familiar, where people get impatient if the service extends a few minutes over the hour! It also made me imagine how difficult it must be for East and West to understand each other.

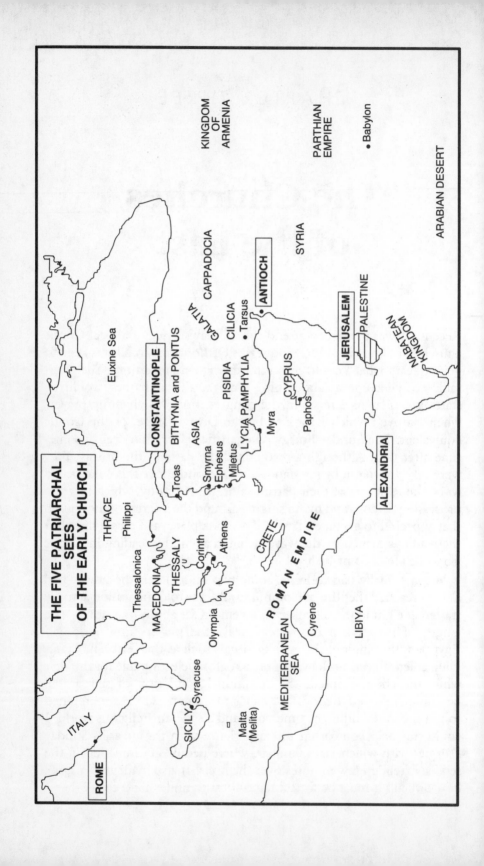

THE FIVE PATRIARCHAL
SEES
OF THE EARLY CHURCH

ROME

ITALY

SICILY • Syracuse

Malta
(Melita)

MEDITERRANEAN
SEA

LIBIYA

Cyrene •

ROMAN EMPIRE

CRETE

Olympia

Athens •

Corinth •

THESSALY

MACEDONIA

Thessalonica

Philippi

THRACE

Euxine Sea

CONSTANTINOPLE

BITHYNIA and PONTUS

ASIA

Troas •

Smyrna •
Ephesus •
Miletus •

LYCIA PAMPHYLIA

PISIDIA

GALATIA

CAPPADOCIA

CILICIA

Tarsus •

ANTIOCH •

SYRIA

Myra •

CYPRUS

Paphos •

JERUSALEM

PALESTINE

NABATEAN KINGDOM

ALEXANDRIA

KINGDOM
OF
ARMENIA

PARTHIAN
EMPIRE

• Babylon

ARABIAN DESERT

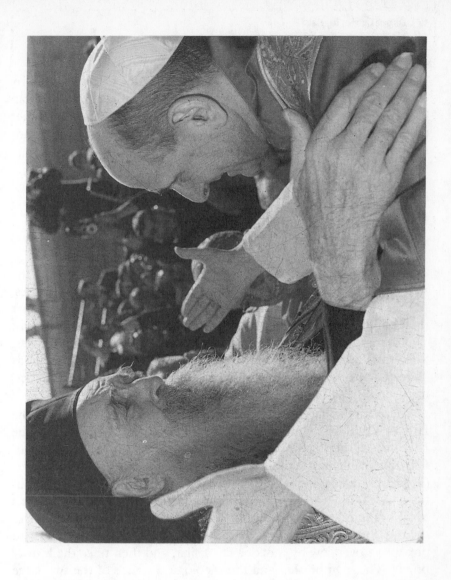

Pope Paul VI and Patriarch Athenagoras. Jerusalem, January 1964.

In seeking therefore to understand something of the Orthodox churches, one has got to bear in mind that there is a big cultural gap between East and West. The story of the East-West Schism (sometimes prejudicially called the 'Eastern' Schism), the first big rift in Christianity, is really all about this lack of understanding.

Origins of the churches of the East

To attempt to unravel the many churches that make up those of the East is no easy task because of their lengthy and complex histories. Another important factor from the westerner's point of view is that these churches often use different titles in various countries and forums. This makes it extremely difficult to track down the individual churches. Some of the older terminology used by westerners, such as "Greater"and "Lesser"(for Eastern and Oriental) Orthodox churches, has been dropped for obvious reasons.

There are two large families of churches within the churches of the East or Orthodox churches, namely the *Eastern* Orthodox and the *Oriental* Orthodox churches, the latter also known as the non-Chalcedonian churches which name gives us a clue as to their origins. (However, in keeping with our criterion of not using negative definitions we should avoid the term non-Chalcedonian as far as possible.) Most of them trace their origins to one of the early Church Councils such as Ephesus (431) or Chalcedon (451). It might be easiest to present an overview by way of a chart first, and then trace the history briefly. The membership and the theological stance of the two large families can be presented schematically as follows:

The two families of Orthodox churches

Eastern Orthodox churches

* Accept seven Ecumenical
  Councils
* Accept Chalcedonian Christology

Oriental Orthodox churches

* Accept three Ecumenical
  Councils
* Express understanding of
  Christology in slightly
  different ways to the
  Eastern Orthodox

Member churches

Patriarchates:
  Constantinople
  Alexandria
  Antioch
  Jerusalem
  Moscow
  Belgrade
  Bucharest
  Sophia

Other autocephalous[1] churches:
  Cyprus
  Greece
  Georgia
  Poland
  Czechoslovakia
  Albania
  Mt Sinai

Autonomous churches:
  Finland
  Latvia
  Lithuania
  Japan
  America[3]

Member churches

Armenian
Coptic
Syrian
Ethiopian
Malankara Syrian
    Orthodox Church of India

Assyrian Church of the East[2]

Eastern Orthodox churches and the background to the East-West Schism

Let us firstly consider the larger of the two families, namely, the Eastern Orthodox churches which today number 139 million throughout the world.

History books tell us that the separation from Western Christianity took place in 1054, but things were not quite as simple as that. Tensions had been building up over some centuries. In order to understand these tensions we need to delve into the history behind the East-West Schism. In brief, the differences between East and West were political, social, cultural and theological. Some or all of these elements combined in the individual events which go to make up the history of the relationship that unfortunately resulted in the definitive break of 1054. In order to form a better idea of these events, it is necessary to go back a little in time before then.

The spread of Islam

The Middle Ages appeared to be a time when the Christian Church was united. But in fact, by the year 700 Christendom was beginning to lose to Islam a large part of the lands that had been Christian for hundreds of years. Islamic expansion was advancing in North Africa, Syria, Palestine and Spain. As a result of this spread of Islam, three of the five ancient Patriarchal Churches (cf. map on page 44) disappeared as forces in Christendom—Alexandria, Antioch, and Jerusalem. This left Constantinople and Rome. It meant that the West knew little or nothing about the earliest bishoprics of the ancient world. (Unfortunately this ignorance has persisted so that many in the Western churches today know very little about the Orthodox. Indeed many in the West received a religious education which was silent on the very existence of the Eastern churches.)

This disappearance of three Patriarchal Sees meant that Christendom was shared, if you like, between Rome and Constantinople. In 700, of course, they did not see themselves as rivals as they were part of a single political unity, namely the Christian Empire. The Emperor of Constantinople was the ruler of large parts of Italy including Rome. Byzantine officials were a common sight in the streets of Rome. Ravenna was the capital of Byzantine government and its beautiful mosaics attest to its Byzantine heritage in a striking way to this day.

The ecumenical flavor of Rome can be seen in the origin of the popes around that time. If one takes, for example, the century from 654 to 752, in which there were seventeen popes, the following breakdown is revealed:

- 5 were Roman;
- 5 were Syrian;
- 3 were Greek;
- 3 came from Sicily (Greek);
- 1 came from an unknown part of Italy.[4]

From this it can be seen that eleven of the seventeen popes had a Greek rather than a Latin background. This was not the case in the century prior to 650, so that one can say there were positive gains in terms of the ecumenical nature of Rome after the loss of Jerusalem, Antioch and Alexandria.

During this period relationships between the Greek emperors and the popes were reasonably good. The emperor was well received in Rome and the pope likewise in Constantinople. The popes had also given support to Councils held in the East by sending legates to Councils such as was done in 681 for the Third Council of Constantinople. But clearly, even at this early time, it was well known that Constantinople acknowledged the primacy of Rome and saw itself as "equal to Rome after Rome".

However, during the seventh century and later, factors were at work undermining the unity and harmony of East and West. Each event can be seen as minor in itself, but collectively and accumulatively, they gained a momentum that eventually broke the Christian Church in two in 1054. For the next 900 years (but for two brave attempts at the Councils of Lyons and Ferrara-Florence) the relationship between East and West was virtually dead. It was eventually resuscitated by the meeting of Pope Paul VI and Patriarch Athenagoras I in Jerusalem in January 1964.

Unity or Uniformity

But let us return to the story. An early incident that can be seen as typical of the mistrust between East and West that was beginning to be felt, was the case of Theodore, Archbishop of Canterbury. He was appointed by the pope in 668 to the see of Canterbury, but because he was Greek-speaking, the pope also sent Hadrian, an abbot from Naples, to keep an eye on him in case he tried to introduce Greek customs contrary to the "true Faith" into the church in England.

Theodore himself noted some of the differences in customs between Romans and Greeks:

The Romans reconciled penitents within the apse of the church, but the Greeks did not; ... the Greeks excommunicated those who failed to receive communion for three successive Sundays, but the Romans did not; ... Roman monks had slaves, but Greek monks did not; ... the Greeks accepted widows as nuns, but the Romans did not.[5]

These kinds of differences raised problems for the believers relating to the unity of the two branches of the Christian Church. If different customs were allowed, how could discipline be preserved and how soon would doctrinal differences follow? The ancient but ever-new problem of maintaining unity in diversity, and not confusing a soulless uniformity with unity, was exposed in a practical way.

When considering the incipient mistrust between East and West, it is important to remember that although the Western Latin culture was initially thought to be inferior to the Eastern Greek culture, the West did have the drawcard of the city of Rome which had become the centre of Christendom and to which Christians flocked. Monks and bishops from the West travelled to Rome to find authority, learning and advice. This may have created among some Romans the opinion that Rome was superior to the East in other ways as well. Looking at history there is no doubt that feelings of superiority and arrogance on the part of Rome were manifest from time to time, greatly offending the people of the East who had, after all, passed on Christianity to the West in the first place.

The iconoclastic movement

The next important step in the events leading up to 1054 centred around what is known as the iconoclastic movement (the drive to get rid of sacred images and icons in worship), which dominated the Constantinople church from 726 to 787. In 729, the Greek emperor sent Gregory II an instruction forbidding pictures of martyrs and angels to be hung in the churches under his jurisdiction. The pope reacted strongly to being told what to do in religious matters and described the event as a breach of faithfulness to Peter and Rome. This incident provides yet another example of the growing friction between East and West.

After this clash the pope tended to turn more and more to the West for support, to such places as those we now call England, France and

Germany. Let us quote two incidents indicative of this development. We know, for example, that in the winter of 753–4 and the following spring, Pope Stephen III travelled from Rome to Saint Denis, outside Paris, and there on 28 July 754 crowned Pepin the Short as King of the Franks (the first of the Carolingian kings) and appointed his two sons, Charlemagne and Carloman, as his joint heirs.[6] Thus he established an ally against the emperors in Constantinople and the Longobards in northern Italy. The second incident is the crowning by the pope of Charlemagne as emperor of the West in 800. The pope had now become a political figure in the West, on whom the kings of Europe would rely for support. This event was a two-edged sword for it simultaneously signalled the political liberation of the West as well as, ultimately, the religious disruption of Christendom.

The *filioque* clause

The adoption of the *filioque* clause in the creed was yet another incident that served to aggravate the estrangement between East and West. It is necessary to briefly give the historical background to this small phrase which has had consequences that have reverberated down the centuries. The First Council of Constantinople (381) resolved a very controversial matter of doctrine pertaining to the creed, later to resurface in the context of the *filioque* (meaning "and from the Son") clause. The council decreed that the Holy Spirit proceeds "from the Father".

In the West, possibly in Spain in the seventh century, someone added "and from the Son", so that the relevant part of the creed read: "The Holy Spirit who proceeds from the Father *and (from) the Son*". Charlemagne soon accepted this into the Mass, partly perhaps to show his independence of the East. He saw to it that it was implemented throughout the West although the popes themselves never used it until the eleventh century! Again, this development was typical of a papacy that was aligning itself more and more with the Latin West. In this case it was also not prepared to abide by the earlier Council of Nicea. This action could be understandably interpreted by the East as arrogant and showing complete disregard for the ancient tradition of the Church.

Further proof of the pro-Western alignment of the popes in these centuries can be seen by looking at the nationalities of the popes. In the years from 752 to 1054 there were 44 Roman-born popes, 11 Italians, 4 Germans, 1 Frenchman and 1 Sicilian. Clear enough evidence of the political leanings of the papacy!

The *filioque* clause was controversial, but in fact, not an insurmountable problem. As late as 1050, Pope Leo IX could defend either phrasing of the creed:

A fruit may be said to come from the trunk of a tree, or from the branch, or from the trunk through the branch; so the Spirit may be said to come from the Father, or from the Son, or from the Father through the Son.[7]

It is worth noting that in 1988, the Anglican bishops of the world urged their churches to omit the *filioque* clause from the creed in acknowledgement of the above unfortunate historical events.

The Bulgarian bungle

The next significant event concerns squabbles over missionary territory and Roman heavy-handedness. Boris of Bulgaria (852–907) had approached the Franks in the West and asked for missionaries to be sent to his people. Constantinople got wind of this, and maintaining that it was their territory, sent Constantine (alias Cyril 826–869) and Methodius (815–885) to help out. (Boris became a "Constantinople" Christian in 865.) They together created an alphabet in which the Slavonic languages could be written, called the Glagolitic Script. They also developed a simpler version called Cyrillic. Naturally they encouraged liturgies using the native languages. This displeased Rome, which had insisted on Latin in the West and regarded the languages of the barbarians as "uncouth, uncultured and unwritten". (The Eastern Emperor, Michael III, in turn thought Latin "a barbarian and Scythian tongue".)

On the other hand, the Orthodox Church imposed its own kind of rituals on the Slavs and this, together with its refusal to grant autonomy to the Bulgarian Church, encouraged Boris in 866 to find out what sort of a deal he might strike with Rome and Nicholas I. The kind of questions he asked Nicholas I were of a very practical nature:

Were the Byzantines right to forbid the Bulgars to take baths on Wednesdays and Fridays? To take communion without wearing their belts? To eat the meat of animals killed by eunuchs? Was it true that no layman could conduct public prayers for rain, or make a sign of the cross over a table before a meal? And that lay-folk must stand in church with arms folded over their breast? ("No, no, no", said the Pope.) Were the Greek clergy right to refuse to accept the repentance of some of the pagan rebels? ("Of course not", said the Pope.)[8]

His questions also give us a glimpse of the life of a Christian living in a pagan society in the Dark Ages and the kind of religious questions with which they were preoccupied:

How many times in the year should one fast? When should one breakfast on non-fasting days? Is sex permissible on Sundays? Should one take communion every day in Lent? What animals and birds might a Christian eat? Should women cover their heads in church? Can you work on Sundays and feastdays? What should one do when a military campaign coincides with Lent? Or when news of an enemy attack interrupts prayers? How can soldiers on campaign perform their religious duties? Was Christian charity compatible with punishing murderers, thieves, and adulterers? Could torture be used? Might criminals claim asylum in church? How should one treat disobedience or cowardice in the army? What about frontier guards who let fugitives escape—was there an alternative to the death sentence?[9]

Finally, to bring the negotiations to an end, Cyril and Methodius travelled to Rome to try and iron out particular problems of liturgy and territory. Fortunately Nicholas I had died, for his successor, Hadrian II, took a favourable stand on their work and permitted the use of Slavonic liturgy in a bull (867–8). This appeared to bring the incident to a happy end, but later (880), John VIII imposed a qualified ban on Slavonic. Unfortunately after John VIII, all popes banned the use of local tongues, thus locking the Western Church into the Latin language and a certain mentality. Because of the inflexibility of the West, Bulgaria and the Slav world eventually turned to the East.

The Photius fracas

There was worse to follow in the deteriorating East-West relationship. In 858, the Patriarch of Constantinople, Ignatius, was forced to resign when his empress, Theodora, was overthrown. Ignatius was seen as being too intransigent towards the iconoclast clergy who sought readmittance to the Church. So Photius, regarded by the Greek Church as a saint and scholar, was elected his successor. But Pope Nicholas I, two years later, refused to recognize Photius, declared his election uncanonical, excommunicated him, and reinstated Ignatius. The Byzantine world simply ignored this decision, regarding it as a blatant intrusion by the pope into the internal affairs of the Eastern Church.

To rub salt in the wound, in 867 Photius convened a council at Constantinople (to which papal legates were not admitted) and denounced Latin errors, including the *filioque* addition to the creed. However, on the accession of Basil I, Photius lost his backing, and Ignatius was restored, but on the latter's death in 877, Photius became patriarch once again, this time with approval of Pope John VIII! This unhappy incident further shows the ongoing and deteriorating jurisdictional problems between East and West. Over the next two centuries, although there were no major clashes, there was a general drifting apart. The pope was no longer informed of the election of the Patriarch of Constantinople. After 1012 he was also removed from the prayers of the Eastern rite.[10]

The events of 1054

The climax to the breakdown of the East-West relationship is normally given as the year 1054. The immediate events which led up to the schism are well known.

From around 1040 the papacy decided to impose the Latin rite on the churches of southern Italy (which were Greek by custom). The Normans were to provide the military force if necessary, though the pope soon became nervous of the growing strength of his would-be allies. In Constantinople, Michael Cerularius responded to the pope's initiatives tit for tat, by imposing the Eastern rite on Latin churches in Constantinople and rejecting such western customs as the use of unleavened bread, the celibacy requirement for clergy and the use of the *filioque* clause (the treachery of the West over this latter matter was not forgotten).

In 1052, the bishop of Trani in Apulia, Italy (whose churches were Greek in discipline and customs), received a letter from the metropolitan of Bulgaria, defending the Greek use of leavened bread in the Mass and the practice of fasting on Saturdays. The Bishop of Trani reported this to the pope and western bishops. It caused a huge furore and raised again the problem of Roman jurisdiction versus Greek autonomy and the desire to protect and preserve their distinctive customs.

In this electric environment, in 1054 the pope sent a team of representatives, headed by Cardinal Humbert, to Constantinople to begin negotiations with the Greeks. Humbert, it should be noted, was a Frenchman from Lorraine, keen on reform but very inflexible in character. He also had a limited knowledge of Greek culture. He was unaware, for example, that the Aramaic "Maranatha"(in Greek, μαραν αθα, cf. 1 Corinthians 16:22) meant "Come, Lord"(or the "Lord is coming") and was not an anathema! The Patriarch of Constantinople,

Michael Cerularius, on the other hand, was a monk from Constantinople who proved to be very hostile to the Latins and as stubborn as Humbert.

Humbert and Michael Cerularius never actually met! Far from solving the problem, they only succeeded in inflaming the situation. Humbert left a bull of excommunication dated 16 July 1054 on the altar of the church of Sancta Sophia. In it he praised the emperor, clergy and laity but castigated Cerularius for sowing "an abundant crop of heresies each day in the bosom of the city". His attack was uncompromising:

> Michael, after having received the written admonitions of our master, Pope Leo, has refused to amend all these errors and many other culpable acts ... Let Michael the neophyte, who improperly bears the title of patriarch ... and with him Leo, who calls himself bishop of Achridia, and Michael's chancellor, Constantine ... and all those who follow them in the abovementioned errors and presumptuous temerities, let all those come under the anathema, Maranatha, with the Simonians.[11]

The bull, which contained many false accusations, was burned by order of Emperor Constantine IX after trying in vain to reconcile the parties. In due course, and by way of retaliation, a synod in Constantinople excommunicated Humbert and his associates.

The Fourth Crusade

However seriously one may view the events of 1054, it was the disastrous Fourth Crusade (1202–1204) which finally torpedoed any hopes of reunification. The problem was that the Fourth Crusade, initiated by Innocent III, got out of hand. A young Byzantine prince pretender, Alexius IV, offered the crusaders great rewards if they would put him on the throne in Constantinople. So the crusaders attacked and captured the city. However, shortly after Alexius' installation, he was murdered in a revolt and one of the conspirators enthroned in his place. This resulted in another wave of pillage, sacrilege, destruction and crimes of every kind.

The upshot of all this was that a westerner, Balwin of Flanders, was placed on the imperial throne and Constantinople became a Latin church. This outrage was indelibly stamped on the Byzantine memory, and in a way, is more definitive in the history of the East-West Schism than the events of 1054. When Michael Paleologus seized power and recaptured Constantinople in 1261 the split was beyond repair as far as the Greeks were concerned.

The contemporary scene

It is not strictly correct to say the Fourth Crusade put paid to all hope of reconciliation. Some attempts at reconciliation were subsequently made as we saw when discussing the Councils of Lyons and Ferrara-Florence in Chapter Two. However, later doctrinal and papal developments only widened the gap between East and West, as did the secession of the Uniat churches from Constantinople to Rome.

It was only on 6 January 1964, that Paul VI and Patriarch Athenagoras I embraced in Jerusalem in a public gesture symbolic of their willingness to repair the damage. Together they read the prayer of Jesus for unity in Chapter 17 of John's gospel. A year later, on 7 December 1965, simultaneously in Rome and Istanbul (the present name for Constantinople), the mutual excommunications of 1054 were officially withdrawn. In the joint declaration the elders of the East and West stated that they:

> Regret the offensive words, unfounded reproaches and unworthy actions which on both sides marked or accompanied the unfortunate events of the period ... Regret equally and efface from the memory and the presence of the Church the Sentences of Excommunication that followed them, the memory of which acts to our own day are an obstacle to our drawing together in charity, and consign them to oblivion ... Deplore lastly the unfortunate precedents and later developments which, influenced by various factors such as misunderstanding and mutual distrust, led in the end to the actual breaking off of ecclesiastical communion.[12]

Commenting on this historic occasion Congar notes that "the bad memories and the mistrust were replaced by feelings of brotherly love; the creed of separation was replaced by the creed of love; the dialogue of charity had begun. However, from that time on it has been ballasted with a theology of extreme importance, that of sister churches".[13]

The current theological dialogue, begun in 1980, between the Roman Catholic Church and the Orthodox Church is a sign of the continuing goodwill on both sides. We shall return to this relationship in a later chapter. For the moment let us consider the other family of Orthodox churches.

Oriental Orthodox churches

The first family of churches was the Eastern Orthodox churches whose origins we have just discussed. The second family, a much smaller family, is that of the Oriental or Ancient Churches (for details cf. Appendix C). They are older than the Eastern Orthodox churches, but less well known, possibly because they have fairly small numbers of members. In order to understand their origins one must, once again, go back to the history surrounding the Councils of Ephesus and Chalcedon.

The Council of Ephesus defined some articles of faith relating to Christology. It defined that Christ was both God and man, but one divine person. Christ had two natures, human and divine, which were united in him in a special way called the "hypostatic" union. Mary too was proclaimed to be, Θεοτοκος (theotokos), the Mother of God. Nestorius, who was Patriarch of Constantinople, is alleged to have held that God merely dwelt in the human nature assumed by him, and that Mary was the Mother of Christ but not of God. For these reasons he was deposed by the Council, but his followers continued in some numbers. The Assyrian Church of the East are said by westerners to be Nestorian, and the Coptic, Syrian and Armenian churches are referred to as Monophysite, as we will explain below. Today in the Middle East and America, Nestorians number about 190,000.[14]

At Chalcedon (451) there was another break within the Christian Church. The Council defined Christ as being perfect God and perfect man in two natures—without confusion, without change, without separation, without division—both natures being united in one person in the hypostatic union. The Monophysites, as their name indicates, allegedly speak of one nature only. (Today we realize that they have been largely misrepresented, cf. Chapter Six). So-called Monophysites continue as Christians in various parts of the world. Today they number altogether about 33,500,000.[15]

We have mentioned the two families of Orthodox churches. But the scene is even more complicated than that! There are Eastern churches that are united to Rome. They became united to Rome at different times down the centuries (cf. diagram on page 28). In some cases not all of a particular church united with Rome, thus bringing about a situation of half the church remaining Orthodox and the other half uniting with Rome. Thus, for example, the Armenian Church has two halves, so to speak, the Armenian Church, united to Rome, and the Armenian Apostolic Church, which belongs to the family of the Oriental Orthodox churches. The Ukrainian Church has a part which is united to Rome and a part which is not—the Ukrainian Orthodox Church.

The Eastern Churches that are united to Rome are sometimes called the Uniat churches, a name which they themselves do not like as it has pejorative overtones. They can be listed as follows, with the dates of union with Rome given in brackets: Maronite (Antioch; 1181); Melkites (Damascus; 1724); Ruthenians (1646 in Czechoslovak), Catholic Greeks (1860), Rumanians, Bulgarians (1595); Italo-Albanians; Catholic-Chaldeans (Babylon; 1552); St Thomas Christians of Malabar Coast (1599); Catholic Armenians (Cilicia; 1740); Catholic Copts (Alexandria; 1739); Catholic Syrian (Antioch; 1662); Catholic Ethiopian (19th century); and Polish Ukrainians (1595). The total number given for these Catholic Eastern (Uniat) churches is about 10 million.[16]

What we have in this chapter is the story of the first great rift in Christianity, the East-West Schism, which resulted in the beginnings of Eastern Orthodox churches, the larger of the two Orthodox families of churches. It is an account of the gradual estrangement of two parts of the same Christian Church that grew apart through a series of unfortunate incidents. That they are talking to each other again is one of the miracles of the ecumenical movement. In the terminology of Irenaeus, they are once again seen as "sister churches"(rather than mother and daughter), or, in the words of Congar, as the "two lungs of the one church".

The Orthodox churches have preserved certain emphases and practices in their tradition which are different to the West. One thinks of their great emphasis on the Church Fathers and Scriptures. One also thinks of their emphasis on the Trinity and the Holy Spirit, both in their theology and praxis. In their eucharistic liturgies ("sacred mysteries"), they have maintained the sense of mystery, *mystagogia*, especially obvious in the iconostasis. One also thinks of their devotion to Mary, *theotokos*, the Mother of God, and their lavish use of rich icons, which they describe as "windows onto heaven"and their fierce adherence to patriarchates and the autonomy of local churches. In dialogues with the Orthodox, as we will see in a later chapter, these characteristics come to the fore in one way or another.

From sketching the first major rift, the East-West Schism, we must now move on to the second big rupture in Christianity, namely, the Protestant Reformation of the sixteenth century.

* * *

Discussion questions

1. Do you have any experience of, or contact with, the Orthodox churches? What have you learned about them?

2. Do you think that language and customs are a barrier to Christian unity? How do you see the difference between unity and uniformity?

3. What can the Churches of the West learn from the Orthodox traditions?

For further reading:

The Orthodox churches

Bria, I., *The Sense of Ecumenical Tradition, The Ecumenical Witness and Vision of the Orthodox*, Geneva, WCC, 1991.

Harkaniakis, S., *The Orthodox Church and Catholicism*, Sydney, Australian Council of Churches, c. 1975.

Limouris, G. (ed.), *Justice, Peace and Integrity of Creation: Orthodox Insights*, Geneva, WCC, 1990.

—— *Icons: Windows on Eternity*, Geneva, WCC, 1990.

Lossky,V., *The Mystical Theology of the Eastern Churches*, London, Clarke, 1957.

Meyendorff, J., *The Orthodox Church*, New York, St Vladimir's Seminary Press, 1981.

—— *Byzantine Theology*, London, Mowbrays, 1975.

Robertson, R., *The Eastern Christian Churches*, Rome, Editioni Orientalia Christiana, 1988.

Staniloe, D., *Theology and the Church*, New York, St Vladimir's Seminary Press, 1980.

Ware, K., *The Orthodox Way*, Oxford, Mowbray, 1979.

Ware, T., *The Orthodox Church*, Harmondsworth, Penguin, 1963.

Notes

1. This word means independent or self-governing. It is used of churches that appoint their own chief bishop.
2. Not strictly speaking an Oriental Orthodox church. cf. Appendix C.
3. Cf. for this list of Eastern Orthodox churches: P. Meagher, et al., (eds), *Encyclopedic Dictionary of Religion*, Vol. A to E, Washington, Corpus Publications, 1979, p. 1144 and E. Finn, *These Are My Rites*, Collegeville, Liturgical Press, 1980. The churches of North America and Japan are not officially recognized by the body of Eastern Orthodox churches.
4. Cf. R. Southern, *Western Society and the Church in the Middle Ages*, Harmondsworth, Penguin, 1970, p. 54.
5. Ibid., p. 57.
6. Cf. Einhard & Notker the Stammerer, *Two Lives of Charlemagne*, trans. by L. Thorpe, Harmondsworth, Penguin, 1969, p. 3.
7. Ibid., p. 67.
8. Cf. P. Johnson, *A History of Christianity*, Harmondsworth, Penguin, 1976, p. 181. For an account of Cyril and Methodius also see S. Neill, *A History of Christian Missions*, Harmondsworth, Penguin, 1964.
9. Ibid., p. 182.
10. Cf. J. Holmes & B. Bickers, *A Short History of the Catholic Church*, London, Burns and Oates, 1983, p. 65. Other useful references are: T. Bokenkotter, *A Concise History of the Catholic Church*, New York, Doubleday, 1977 and D. Knowles & D. Obolensky, *The Christian Centuries*, Vol. Two, London, DLT, 1969.
11. Ibid., p. 65.
12. Ibid., p. 66.
13. Cf. Y. Congar, *Diversity and Communion*, London, SCM Press, 1984, p. 86.
14. This figure is taken from D. Barrett (ed.), *World Christian Encyclopedia*, Nairobi & London, OUP, 1982, p. 817.
15. Ibid., Armenian: 3,350,600; Coptic: 7,918,500; Malankara Syrian (Syro-Malabarese): 2,811,100; Ethiopian: 17,333,000; Syrian Jacobite: 1,811,100.
16. Ibid., p. 825.

CHAPTER FOUR

The Protestant Churches and the Roman Catholic Church

When one enters a Protestant church, one might be struck, for example, by the prominence of a huge, imposing pulpit, or the plainness of the table at the front, or the lack of holy pictures and crucifixes around the walls. The explanation of these emphases lies in their history and theology. For this reason there is a great need for those unfamiliar with Protestantism to become acquainted with the original story and inspiration behind men like Luther, Calvin, Zwingli, Knox and Henry VIII in order to understand Protestant churches today. Conversely, those not familiar with the Roman Catholic Church need to get to know it better. The Vatican II *Decree on Ecumenism* encourages all Christians to get to know other Churches by studying "their history, spiritual and liturgical life, their religious psychology and cultural background".

This is what we are trying to do on a very modest scale. It might be somewhat easier getting to know the Protestant churches or the Roman Catholic Church rather than the Orthodox, as the former have been part and parcel of western society since the sixteenth century.

Who are Protestants? Where did they come from? How are they different from Roman Catholics and Orthodox Christians? As was mentioned above, the Protestant churches are the result of the most recent major rift in Christianity, namely the sixteenth century Reformation (cf. diagram on page 28).

The Renaissance

Before outlining the causes of the Reformation, it is useful and necessary to place the whole religious upheaval called the Reformation in the context of a larger European movement known as the Renaissance, or Rebirth, which occurred in the fifteenth and sixteenth centuries. It was a movement that was characterized by a general cultural transition involving political, religious, economic and social changes.

Europe was experiencing great changes during this time. Looking at the political scene, states, in the modern sense, were beginning to emerge. In general, there was a movement of states to assert themselves from under the shadow of either the papacy or the Holy Roman Empire which in fact, was neither holy nor Roman. The end of the Hundred Years War (1453) helped to delineate France and England. France under Francis I was emerging in its own right and, by the Treaty of Bologna (1516), obtained the right to appoint all bishops and abbots in its kingdom. In Spain, the capture of Granada marked the end of the recapture of territory from the Arabs and the final unification of Spain.

In the East, Poland, which stretched from Lithuania to the Ukraine, marked the boundary between Latin Christianity and the Orthodox. Moscow became the third Rome. The Patriarch of Constantinople finally recognized the independence of the Russian Orthodox Church and consecrated the Patriarch of Moscow in 1589.

In the Holy Roman Empire, since 1438, the emperor had always been chosen from the Hapsburg family, but in 1519, Charles V was elected, inheriting the kingdom of Spain, the domain of Burgundy, as well as Habsburg territory. With the voyages of discovery, the dream of conquering the whole world suddenly seemed possible.

This era is also known as the period of the Voyages of Discovery. Batholomew Dias rounded the Cape of Good Hope in 1487 and gave promise of finding a route to the East. Vasco da Gama in 1497 brought that hope to fruition by discovering a way to the spice-rich East. In a voyage that started in 1519, Magellan sailed westwards from Europe around the tip of South America (Cape Horn) and by circumnavigating the globe proved that believers in the flat earth were wrong. Christopher Columbus discovered the West Indies in 1492, and opened a whole new chapter in the history of colonization, commercial and cultural exploitation, and Christianization. New peoples with strange cultures were encountered, giving rise to all sorts of questions about their humanity, customs and ways of evangelising them. In many ways the new knowledge, exciting discoveries and resultant questions can be paralleled to the discoveries of the contemporary space age.

In the commercial world, capitalism was growing during this period. After the crusades, trade with the East picked up again and the riches flowed through the Mediterranean ports and cities like Venice and Genoa. Not only was there an accumulation of commercial goods, but banks, institutions and individuals began to accumulate capital. The Christian Church's stand against usury (interest) began to crumble in the sixteenth century and the reality of a changed commercial world became evident. (In England as early as 1197, interest had been prohibited on religious grounds. Elsewhere it was limited to 5 or 10%. In spite of papal bulls condemning usury as late as 1586, some theologians were arguing for a change while the laity continued to do business as if the teaching did not exist.)

The world of art, science and literature was in upheaval as well. This new learning was characterized by a rebirth of letters and arts, and by a return to classical Greek and Roman writers. People who led this movement where called humanists, and included Desiderius Erasmus, Niccolo Machiavelli, Thomas More, Cardinal Wolsey, and Albrecht von Bonstetten in Switzerland.

The spirit of the Renaissance was captured in the Latin slogan *ad fontes* ("return to sources")—much like ecumenism today! The humanists were able to show, for example, that papal documents establishing papal supremacy were spurious, and that the Vulgate Bible was not always correct in its translations of the Greek or Hebrew originals. Erasmus produced an annotated translation of the New Testament from the Greek in 1516. The Church Fathers were studied and used in a new light. All this new learning had an unsettling effect on many who saw their ideas and religion challenged. To make matters worse the printing press was discovered in Europe by Guttenberg in 1457 (it had been discovered in China and Korea in the thirteenth and fourteenth centuries respectively) and played a significant role in the dissemination of all these new, so-called "Protestant" ideas.

The era of the Reformation was therefore a time of new learning, fresh ideas, the challenge and overthrow of many old worldviews and the excitement of new intellectual, commercial and religious horizons.

What were the causes of the Reformation?

Having just reflected on the larger picture of society during the Renaissance, we can now consider the condition of the Christian Church at that time. From the description of the incidents leading to the East-West Schism in the previous chapter, one can see that there were some aspects of the Western Church that needed reform, review or correction. One obvious example would be the jurisdictional powers of Rome and how they were exercised.

A range of things about the Church of the sixteenth century needed reform. They related to clerical bureaucracy, taxation, dispensations from church law, indulgences, papal involvement in warfare, the moral lives of priests and bishops, the denial of the cup at the eucharist, etc. In other words, we can say the need for reform touched on moral, legal, administrative, doctrinal and liturgical matters.

That the Church should need to be reformed should not surprise us, as it is a human as well as a divine institution. The human aspect ensures that it will always need correction or reform. Vatican II in fact stated outright that the Church must be always renewing or reforming itself. The task is never completed, as the phrase went, *Ecclesia reformata, semper reformanda* ("The reformed Church is always in need of reform"). As a result of the events of the sixteenth century, some Protestant churches have called themselves the "Reformed" churches, while we know that many religious orders in the Roman Catholic Church generated reformed, breakaway groups which thought the original order needed radical reform.

If one thinks of the Christian Church today there might be some things that spring to mind as needing reform. How good, for example, is our preaching today? Are our liturgies prayerful and attractive? Is the Church too hung up on money matters? Are the clergy devoted to their ministry or more interested in secular matters? Are lay people willing, and being invited, to share their gifts and talents with the community? Should celibacy for ministers be optional in those churches where it is currently compulsory? Should the pool of candidates for ordination include women where it presently does not?

So the question of reform is perennial. But here we want to focus on the Protestant Reformation. A study of what was wrong with the Christian Church at that time is essential.

We can begin by highlighting the failure of pastors in general to lead their followers by example, in spite of repeated calls to reform. To that extent the emphasis is on moral reform although the immediate cause of Luther's concern in 1517 was the doctrinal matter of indulgences.

It was often individual incidents that highlighted the need for moral reform. As Chadwick points out:

A priest who was observed to be publicly drunken in the taverns was allowed to continue his ministry without rebuke; the scandal was notorious; and it was hardly noticed that in some other cases of drunkenness pastoral discipline was enforced. A corporation engaged in a suit over property with a monastery found settlement to be impossible without such an expenditure of time and money as rendered the distant verdict futile. A cleric known to be guilty of homicide was seen to escape with a modest imprisonment on bread and water. A parish priest kept a concubine openly and was unrebuked. An illiterate devoid of any knowledge of the Latin tongue was ordained to the priesthood, and could be heard mumbling nonsensically through his prayers at the altar; and the parishioners knew nothing of learned and devout men whom elsewhere bishops might be ordaining. Too many scandals; too many inconveniences; too many injustices; too much inefficiency unremedied and apparently irremediable—these lent force to the cry of churchman and of politician for reformation.[1]

The non-residence of pastors

Inevitably people noticed irregularities with the clergy as, in a way, they were the most visible part of the local church. The non-residence of parish priests and bishops was often a big problem; for example, the bishop of Worcester in England was an Italian who was resident in, and engaged by, the Vatican court in Rome! Linacre, Henry VIII's physician, prior to being ordained priest, had been rector of four parishes, a canon of three cathedrals and precentor of York Minster! Cardinal della Rovere (later Julius II), held at one time the archbishopric of Avignon, the bishoprics of Bologna, Lausanne, Coutances, Viviers, Mende, Ostia, and Velletri, and the abbacies of Nonantola and Grottaferrata.[2]

Another shocking and amusing example is that of Antoine du Prat, the French diplomat, who was made Archbishop of Sens in France and entered his cathedral for the first time in his funeral procession! Cardinal Ippolito d'Este, Archbishop of Milan (1520–50) never once visited his city!

The non-residence of priests obviously had serious consequences. Why then did they choose not to live in their parishes? Some it seems, became the title holder of a benefice while studying at a university removed from the titular parish, or simply because the priest preferred to live in a particular town and receive the income from his benefice. Thus many parishes between the fourteenth and seventeenth centuries had no real pastors. Delumeau quotes examples:

In the diocese of Angers in 1413, 103 parishes out of a total of 436, in other words twenty-three per cent, were in the charge of curés who were pursuing university studies far from their flocks. In the deanery of Oudenburg, near Bruges, there were fifty-four curés in 1455 and only twelve resident curés. An unpublished inquiry into the diocese of Sens in 1495 reveals that fifty to sixty per cent of pastors were absent from their parishes: this is more serious than the position at Aix-en-Provence in the early fifteenth century (thirty to forty per cent non-resident), but comparable to the diocese of Narbonne at the same time (fifty-eight per cent). Of 241 parishes in the diocese of Liège, seventy-two curés were without resident pastors in 1501 and ninety-five in 1521; in 1526 nearly half the parishes were staffed by priests who had no charge.[3]

Moral lives of the clergy

To add to this, the clergy were often unworthy and adulterous, although it is obviously difficult to get accurate records of what was happening. One might firstly distinguish between religious orders and the secular clergy.

As regards religious orders, the situation was grave. Of the four orders of friars founded in the thirteenth century, i.e., Franciscans, Dominicans, Carmelites and the Augustinians, all but the last had become scandalously lax in piety and discipline. Being wealthy enough not to have to work hard, they "wandered outside their walls, drank in taverns, and pursued amours".[4] Erasmus declared that many convents of men and women differed little from public brothels. Petrarch, on the other hand, was impressed by the discipline and devotion of the monastery where his brother lived.

In 1503, a papal delegate sent to reform the Benedictine monasteries in France, complained that the monks lived the lives of Bacchanals and were more worldly than the mere worldling. Pope Leo X, in 1516, lamented that kings, princes and laity had all lost their respect for the monks in France because of their corrupt lives. This loss of trust and support among ordinary folk was also due to the fact that the monks were neglecting their traditional works of charity, hospitality and education.

As regards the secular clergy, concubinage was evident. Delumeau, referring to the sixteenth century, puts the proportion of concubinary priests to the whole clergy of the diocese, at about a quarter for the Low Countries, and a third for Rhineland. In England, thousands of priests had concubines, says Durant, and in Germany nearly all. In Rome it was assumed that priests had concubines.

So bad was the situation, so gross the immorality of the clergy that suggestions in favour of allowing priests to marry began to be heard, according to one historian.[5] At the Council of Constance in 1418, Cardinal Zabarella proposed the restoration of clerical marriage if sacerdotal concubinage could not be suppressed. Later on Erasmus was also of this opinion.

Of course there were those on the one hand, who lived dissolute and promiscuous lives, and on the other, the majority who had a loving and faithful relationship with a woman. Some exchanged vows and raised children like married couples. In some cases no attempt was made to hide concubinage and at public festivals the places of honour were given as a matter of course to priests and their consorts.

Potter, reviewing the situation in northern Switzerland prior to the Reformation, notes that "Everyone knew that by paying an appreciable annual sum to the bishop's official at Constance, a priest might cohabit with his housekeeper and raise a family without further action being taken. Some might disapprove, but the whole issue aroused little feeling."[6]

Priests often had to work for a living and thus needed a housekeeper. Now the canonical age of housekeepers was sixty. Given the life expectancy of the period, and the fact that bishops would have had first option on 'canonical' housekeepers, it is not difficult to see what happened. Priests and curés would raise children who would serve at the altar and one day inherit the benefice of their father. If necessary, the dispensation for a bastard child to be ordained could be purchased in Rome. The problem was bad enough for a Council in 1512 to order that priests should at least refrain from turning up at the marriages of their sons and daughters![7]

However one should not overestimate the weight of this morality factor in causing the Reformation. People were understanding and forgiving of the 'sins of the flesh' but harsher on injustices in money matters and inadequate pastoral care. As Delumeau observes:

Inquiries into this aspect of the matter should concentrate more on religious and not moral factors, and ask rather why the Church met the people's religious expectations so inadequately, distributed the sacraments, said mass and prayed so incompetently. Even though priests had women and children, if they had celebrated mass devoutly, been enlightened confessors and above all instructed their people in the catechism, there is every chance that the Protestant Reformation would never have happened.[8]

Corruption in the Church's administration

The Church itself, in its own administration, needed cleaning up. Benefices were sometimes sold or held collectively. Luther mentions a certain court follower in Rome who alone held twenty-two parishes, seven priories, as well as forty-four benefices.[9] Alexander VI created eighty new offices and received 760 ducats from each of the appointees. Julius II, we are told, had a collection of 101 secretaries who collectively paid him 74,000 ducats for the privilege, while Leo X collected 202,000 ducats from sixty chamberlains and 141 squires to the papal household! There were also threats of excommunication if debts were not paid. Usury as well as simony was practised. Pardons, masses, candles, ceremonies, curacies, benefices and bishoprics not infrequently had a price on them. It was over the question of "selling" indulgences (pardons) that Luther reacted. As the jingle went: "when the coin in the coffer rings, a soul from Purgatory springs".

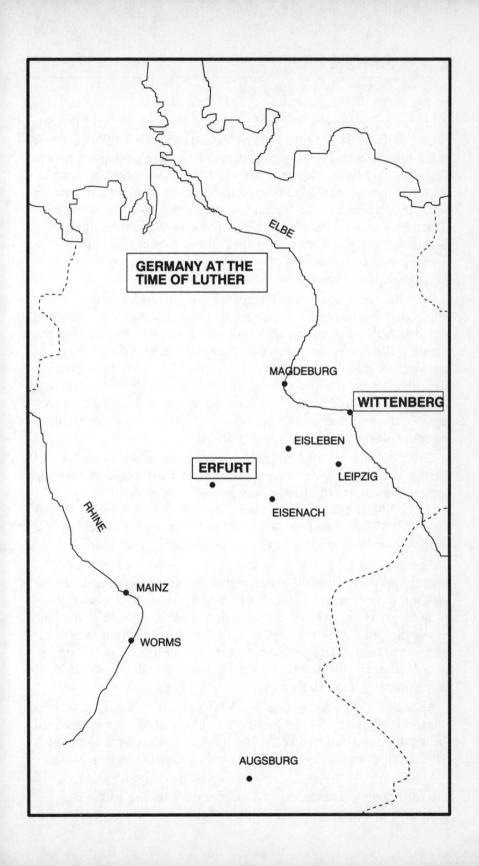

GERMANY AT THE
TIME OF LUTHER

ELBE

MAGDEBURG

WITTENBERG

EISLEBEN

ERFURT

LEIPZIG

EISENACH

RHINE

MAINZ

WORMS

AUGSBURG

Luther complained to the Archbishop of Mainz, Cardinal Albrecht, in a letter dated 31 October, 1517, "not so much about the quacking of the preachers" but "the gross misunderstanding among the people which comes from these preachers and which they spread everywhere among common men". He begged the archbishop to give the matter his fatherly attention and "command the preachers of indulgences to preach in another way".[10] While Tetzel was preaching indulgences in Germany, Sanson was offering them at the city gates of Zurich having been rejected by the bishop of Constance who, among other reasons, didn't like money leaving his diocese![11]

In Wittenberg itself the Elector of Saxony had amassed a vast collection of relics with indulgences attached to them. The collection included "a piece of the burning bush of Moses, nine thorns from the crown, stalks of hay and straw on which the Christ child lay, some of the virgin's milk, and a whole baby (one of those murdered by Herod!)—a sort of Tussaud's chamber of horrors".[12] In England the bishops complained of the "stinking boots, mucky combs ... rotten girdles ... locks of hair, and filthy rags ... set forth and commended unto the ignorant people" as authentic relics.[13]

This gullibility is also seen in the superstitious religious practices of the day. Some Christians were foolish enough to believe that having secured the support of a patron saint by prayer, they were free to "make war, gamble, blaspheme, rob, burn and commit adultery with impunity."[14] Others used St Sebastian as an insurance policy against accidents or the plague, or St Christopher against sudden death.

As regards the Church–State relationship there were matters to be reformed as well. Some states demanded restraint upon papal intervention, upon privileges and exemptions, and upon the right of an outside body to levy taxes. In Spain the sovereigns had the right to control the Inquisition, in France the king secured the right to appoint to higher posts in the Church in France, as was the case in England and Germany. In general terms, the power of sovereigns over the Church was increasing in practice, if not in theory.

After the heady years of Boniface VIII and *Unam Sanctam*, with its extraordinary claims for the papacy, the power of the papacy declined for the next two hundred years. The ineffectiveness of the hierarchy is reflected in this amusing story recounted by Chadwick:

The Cardinal d'Amboise, empowered by the king to conduct a reformation in France, needed fortifying for reform with a Bull (from Pope Alexander VI) giving him full authority as papal legate. Thus armed with weapons from the heads of Church and State, he conducted an admirable reformation of several monastic houses and congregations. In 1501 he determined to reform the Cordeliers at Paris, and commissioned two bishops to visit and reform the house. When the commission arrived, the friars hurried away to the chapel, exposed the blessed sacrament, and began singing psalms. The two bishops waited for four hours and then, frustrated, went away. Next day they came back with the Provost of Paris, a hundred archers, and a band of constables. Again the friars fell to their psalms. They were stopped, and the papal bulls and royal decrees were read to them. They replied by quoting extracts in a contrary sense from their charters and the canon law. After a prolonged deadlock, and a different commission composed of Cordeliers, the Cardinal at last secured a measure of reform in the house.[15]

Alexander VI did nothing to enhance the standing of the papacy, having fathered possibly as many as seven children, and Julius II was keener on leading papal armies into war than minding his flock. He was also intent on building (does that have a familiar ring to it?) and laid the foundations of the present St Peter's in Rome on 18 April 1506. He contracted Raphael to paint the chambers and Michelangelo the Sistine Chapel ceiling.

So worldly was Julius II that Erasmus satired him in an imaginary scene between Julius and St Peter in heaven. St Peter fails to recognize Julius in spite of his triple crown and jewelled pall. Even the silver key he displayed looked nothing like the keys Christ gave Peter! Reflecting the corruption in the Church, Machiavelli noted that Italians were more irreligious and corrupt than others, "because the Church and its representatives set us the worst example".[16] Luther was in Rome in 1509 and no doubt took it all in. He later wrote:

> It is horrible and shocking to see the head of Christendom, who boasts that he is the vicar of Christ and successor of St Peter, going about in such a worldly and ostentatious style that neither king nor emperor can equal or approach him. He claims the title of "most holy" and "most spiritual", and yet he is more worldly than the world itself. He wears a triple crown, whereas the highest monarchs wear but one. If that is like the poverty of Christ and of St Peter, then it is a new and strange kind of likeness![17]

Bishops were criticized by another reformer, Zwingli, for becoming "swaggering squires, offenders, warmongers, usurers, cheats, traitors and deserters".[18]

Doctrinal issues

I mentioned earlier that the new ideas of the Renaissance in Europe had an unsettling effect on many people. This effect had a parallel phenomenon in ecclesiastical circles, namely a certain theological vagueness as regards doctrine and this especially in central Europe and England. This dates back to the thirteenth century and builds up to the Reformers. Theology had in fact deteriorated and become detached from the sacramental life of the people, therefore irrelevant to the lives of the people. Erasmus in a way epitomises this; theology for him had become an intellectual exercise divorced from living out one's Christian life. With this detachment from the life of the people, theology became more vulnerable to all kinds of interpretations such as was the case with the doctrine of the real presence in the eucharist, the meaning of the Mass, and the theology of salvation. Nominalism was one such influence which unsettled the thinking of the time and helped to undermine scholasticism.

Another important factor which I have referred to was the weakening of the authority of the pope. We have seen how the corrupt lives of the clergy in general called for reform. But over and above this, the decline in the pope's authority and of the binding force of his decisions only encouraged the cause of the Reformation. As the pope had become a prince among princes, the public saw no reason why they should not combat him as they did other princes. As the pope's influence decreased, the kings of Europe were gaining more and more power, as we saw at the beginning of the chapter, and nationalism in a vague sort of a way was beginning to form. These developments only helped to create the environment favourable to a direct confrontation with the pope and the Roman Church such as Martin Luther ignited.

Calls for reform

The call to reform was consistently made, and consistently rejected. The Cistercian monks of Cluny, in the twelfth century, are symbolic of the recognition of an urgent need for reform. The Councils of Constance (1414–8), Basel (1431–9) and Lateran (1512–17) all urged the Church to reform itself "in head and members". As Chadwick remarks:

Those Councils gave the idea of reformation such an airing that it could never be forgotten. They talked frankly, clamoured for change, advertised abuses, suggested remedies, evoked claims and an idealism which they had then failed to satisfy. They thereby multiplied discontent. If they failed in their practical aim, they left behind a state of public opinion which was restless, critical, disquieted, impatient, demanding reform in theory, and not always sensible of the practical consequences. In 1496 a Frenchman wrote that in men's conversation no topic was more frequent than that of reform.[19]

Elsewhere in the Church, at a different level, the same issues were taken up. One thinks of the Dominican friar, Savonarola, who made an empassioned plea for reform. The response he was met with was papal suspension, excommunication and finally death by burning in 1498! Religious orders too, such as the Franciscans, took up the question of poverty and riches and the need to follow the gospel more closely. Albigensians, Cathari, Hussites (Czech Brethren), Lollards, Waldensians (some linked up with the Swiss Calvinists in the sixteenth century), all in their own ways, often misguidedly, tried to say the same thing: return to the simplicity of the gospel.

In the Low Countries, the *devotio moderna* sprung up under Gerard Groote (1340–1384)—a movement devoted to living according to the Sermon on the Mount, the followers of which called themselves the Brethren of the Common Life. Thomas à Kempis (1380–1471) is probably their best-known member. He wrote *The Imitation of Christ*—a book noted for its emphasis on peace of soul, purity of thought, simplicity of life, blind obedience and flight from the world. Yet as Grimm noted, this approach had its limitations:

> The mysticism of the Brethren could not, because of its abnegation of society and of reason, bring about the thoroughgoing reforms needed to restore the effectiveness of the Church. Its emphasis upon inner spirituality, however, greatly influenced the Christian humanists and some of the reformers.[20]

In 1532, by which time the Reformation was well under way, Erasmus was still drawing attention to the need to reform the Roman Church. He did not want to abandon his Church. As he protested in his *Hyperaspistes* (1526–7): "I shall bear with this Church until I find a better one ... he does not sail badly who steers a middle course between two evils."[21]

However, in spite of all these attempts at reform the basic call for renewal was not met. And as history teaches us, if widespread and persistent demands for reform are not met, revolution occurs. And this was triggered by the Dominican preacher, Tetzel, "selling" indulgences near Wittenberg in 1517. The rest, as they say, is history.

Here is not the place to give detailed accounts of the progress of the whole Reformation nor lengthy descriptions of all the religious leaders of the sixteenth century. A brief outline of the major reformers, however, will identify the main characters on the stage of religious history in the sixteenth century and the thrust of their reforms. Further reading will be suggested at the end of the chapter.

The leaders of the Reformation

Luther

Martin Luther (1483–1546) is not regarded as a thoroughgoing reformer in the way that Calvin, Zwingli, Farel, Bucer, Melanchthon, Oecolampadius, Knox and others are, but he is the first reformer whose actions ignited the whole of Europe.

He was born at Eisleben in Germany, went to the university of Erfurt and while studying there decided to enter the monastery of Augustinian monks. He became a very observant, if scrupulous, monk in a strict monastery. His 'ninety-five theses' registered his objection to salvation made easy by some preachers of indulgences.

His theses caused a lively debate, but neither the subsequent meeting with Cardinal Cajetan in Augsburg (1518), nor the Diet of Worms (1521) under Charles V, was able to get him to recant. The break with Rome, symbolized by the burning of the papal bull in December 1520, was formalized at the Diet of Worms. After the latter, Luther went into hiding at the Wartburg Castle during which time he translated the New Testament into German. He re-entered public life in March 1522. Wittenberg thus became the centre of a reform movement under Luther which marked the beginning of the Lutheran Church. The official Lutheran Confession of Faith, known as the *Augsburg Confession*, was agreed upon in 1530.

In 1524 Luther married Catherine von Bora, a former nun, raised a number of children in a happy family life and died in 1546, after some years of ill health. He has left us much of his writings, collected now in fifty-five volumes.

His theology was based on the Scriptures and the Fathers, which is not surprising as he lectured in the new university at Wittenberg on the psalms and the Pauline letters, in the period 1513–1518. He had a profound sense of his own unworthiness and of God's majesty. His reading of Paul's letter to the Romans led him to see that it is our faith in God's mercy that allows his grace to justify us, not our efforts or good works. It was because of this insight that he rebelled against the abuses of men like Tetzel who were selling indulgences as if redemption was something to be purchased and applied mechanically. In reaction to this he is alleged to have posted his ninety-five theses on the door of the church in Wittenberg.

He was convinced of the importance of following one's own conscience—a point affirmed by Vatican II—and because of this stance he was not able to retract his writings at the Diet of Worms. But by this time he had been drawn into many doctrinal issues beyond his original concerns, such as authority and the papacy. His followers today, called Lutherans, are found throughout the world and number about 75 million. As a church they have bishops (i.e., they have an episcopal system), but also use the terms "president" and "superintendent" for the same office.

Zwingli

Huldreich Zwingli (1484–1531) and Calvin are the two great Swiss reformers. Zwingli started preaching reform in Zurich about the same time as Luther did in Germany. His ideas might have developed independently of Luther, but they were certainly fanned by the revolt in Wittenberg. There seems to have been a general state of readiness for some kind of reform, and given the state of the Christian Church mentioned above, that is no surprise! One common feature was the return to the Scriptures. Another was the reform of worship. Images and relics were removed, the altar stripped and called a table for the Lord's Supper (the Real Presence rejected), and the whole liturgy simplified with the emphasis on a sermon and prayers.

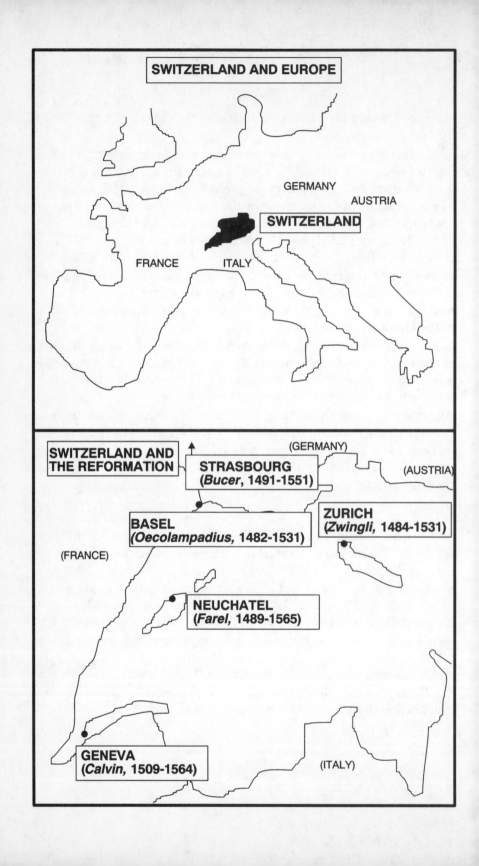

SWITZERLAND AND EUROPE

GERMANY

AUSTRIA

SWITZERLAND

FRANCE   ITALY

SWITZERLAND AND
THE REFORMATION

(GERMANY)

STRASBOURG
(*Bucer*, 1491-1551)

(AUSTRIA)

ZURICH
(*Zwingli*, 1484-1531)

BASEL
(*Oecolampadius*, 1482-1531)

(FRANCE)

NEUCHATEL
(*Farel*, 1489-1565)

GENEVA
(*Calvin*, 1509-1564)

(ITALY)

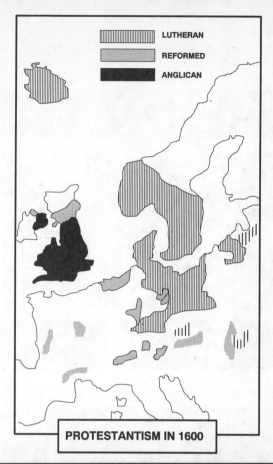

PROTESTANTISM IN 1600

LUTHERAN

REFORMED

ANGLICAN

Geneva Wall of Reformation

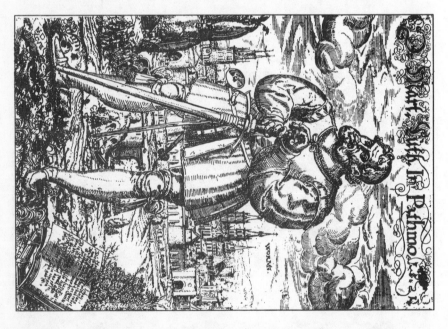

Top: Title page of Bull against Martin Luther and Followers.
Bottom: Luther dressed as a knight.

The visible appearance of the churches and the manner in which services were conducted in Switzerland (Zurich and Geneva) were quite different to those of the Lutherans in Germany. Their worship reflected a more radical theology, and thus these churches became the "Reformed churches".

Zwingli was finally killed in the battle between Zurich and the Catholic cantons. He was succeeded by Henry Bullinger.

Calvin

Jean Calvin (1509–1564), the founder of Calvinism or Presbyterianism, was born in Noyon in France. He studied Latin and theology at the University of Paris and then law at Orleans. A scholarly man, he became a reformer during the year 1532, while in Paris, and had to flee to Switzerland for his life. Passing through Geneva, he was persuaded by Farel to stay. There he became the local preacher and later the pastor, and together with the city council, applied a very strict religious discipline on the city of Geneva. Religious and secular life in Geneva became one under Calvin's regime.

In 1539 he married an Anabaptist widow, Idelette de Bure, who had two children by her first marriage. She and Calvin had one child who unfortunately was born prematurely and died shortly afterwards. Idelette died in 1549 after being sickly for some years. Calvin's delicate health declined rapidly from 1559 until he died on 27 May 1564.

Like Luther, Calvin felt the Christian Church, centred in Rome on the pope, had lost its way, had abandoned the spirit of the gospel and become too worldly. However, he was more radical than Luther in reforming the Christian Church. In 1536 he published his first edition of what became the handbook of Calvinism, *The Institutes of the Christian Religion*. Calvin believed that papal authority was corrupt and thus sought to purify the ministry in the church in Geneva, organizing it along the lines of the primitive church. (Hence the use of four orders—presbyter, elder, deacon and professor—and the use of consistory/presbytery in the Presbyterian and Reformed churches.)

He also placed great emphasis on Scripture which was seen as normative for the Church and rejected the Catholic Mass in its traditional form. As with the iconoclastic movement in the ninth century, all holy pictures and icons were removed. The Lord's Supper was celebrated but less frequently than before and in a simplified manner. Only baptism and eucharist were acknowledged as sacraments. Calvinism is often noted for its doctrine of predestination which refers to

God's preselection of those to be saved and those to be damned, i.e., those chosen for election and those chosen for reprobation. Calvin himself, however, did not give as much attention to this doctrine as others since him have done. In brief, Calvin taught that some are predestined to be saved and others are predestined to be lost. He based his doctrine on Augustine's earlier teaching and evidence in the Scriptures. Life's task is to find out as best one can, if one is saved. Those that are saved show the fruits of this grace in the goodness of their deeds. The problem with this doctrine is that it tended to invalidate free will in a deterministic sort of way.

Henry VIII: The English Reformation

When one thinks of England and the Reformation, one thinks of Henry VIII (1491–1547). However the origin of the Church of England or the Anglicans, is quite different from the Swiss and German experience. Many Anglicans today refer to themselves as Catholics, i.e., Anglo-Catholics. They are not, strictly speaking, part of the "Protestant" churches of the Continent, although for convenience they are often grouped alongside Protestant Churches. Their fight with Rome was of a different nature. Initially it was not doctrinal or over the need for moral reform.

The king in England was not traditionally anti-papal. Far from it. Henry VIII in fact acquired the title of *Fidei Defensor*, bestowed on him by the pope himself, for his defence of the faith on the occasion of the pamphlet Henry wrote against Lutheranism in 1521. But later Henry VIII also wished to get rid of his wife Catherine of Aragon (who had been unable to provide a male heir, the first having died after only seven weeks), and marry Anne Boleyn. He turned to the Church to annul his marriage to Catherine. Henry was unable to persuade Clement VII to do so, so he dismissed Cardinal Wolsey (1529) and started a process of slowly transferring the legal rights and duties of the pope to the crown. In 1532, the Act of Supremacy declared that the king was the head of the Church of England, and Thomas Cranmer (a convinced Reformer) was made the new Archbishop of Canterbury. He annulled Henry's marriage to Catherine, opening the way for Henry to marry Anne Boleyn. In 1535, Bishop Fisher of Rochester and Thomas More, the ex-chancellor, were beheaded for refusing to swear allegiance to the royal supremacy at the cost of their loyalty to papal authority. In the words of Luther: "Junker Heintz will be God and does whatever he lusts".[22]

In the years that followed, the kind of Christianity that was adopted in England varied from a very Reformed/ Presbyterian kind to a milder sort that characterizes much of Anglicanism today. The kind of Christianity varied with the monarch—from a strong Calvinistic influence, as could be seen in the *Book of Common Prayer* and the Thirty-nine Articles, back to Catholicism with Queen Mary. (For example, in 1549, the Strasbourg Reformer, Martin Bucer, accepted Cranmer's invitation to become Regius Professor of Divinity at Cambridge.) Today the liturgy is close to a Roman Catholic liturgy and Anglicans share the same sacraments as Roman Catholics, although sharp differences occur in what are termed "low" Anglican churches. The low churches are much closer to the Reformed churches of the Continent in doctrine and worship.

In the USA, the Episcopalian Church, which derived from the English Anglicans, tended more to the reformed end of the scale. Although they held on to bishops (hence the name episcopal) and priests, they maintained that Scripture was the ultimate rule of faith and adopted two sacraments only, baptism and the Lord's Supper. They use the *Book of Common Prayer* (1928) and the *Hymnal* (1940).

In brief, one could say that the Reformation had a theology that was characterized by an emphasis on justification by faith, on an insistence on the importance of the Scriptures as the Word of God and on authority based on the Bible. It was a theology that rejected transubstantiation and the Mass as sacrifice. It embraced two sacraments, baptism and the Lord's Supper. In their worship, the Reformed churches—the followers of Calvin, Zwingli, Knox and the Puritans— would only follow customs that were laid down in the New Testament. They rejected medieval vestments and ceremonies. The Lutherans and Anglicans, on the other hand, adopted church structures such as bishops, or customs such as vestments, Saints' Days and other local traditions that, although not specifically mentioned in the Scriptures, were not opposed to the gospel.

The Roman Catholic Church

The origins of the Protestant churches are fairly clear, but sometimes people ask: when did the Roman Catholic Church start? The answer is that it is best to think of one Christian (Western) Church at the time of the Reformation, which then split up into the Protestant and Roman Catholic churches. This is not entirely accurate because the Christian Church was called *universal* or *catholic* from the second century, but it is true to say that after the Protestant Reformation, the term *Roman Catholic Church* took on a slightly different meaning, that is, a church centred in Rome that was not one of the Protestant churches (cf. chart on page 28).

The Roman Catholic Church follows the gospel, adheres to the early Church councils and creeds and has seven sacraments, namely, baptism, confirmation, eucharist, penance, holy orders, matrimony and the anointing of the sick. It is a church of Word and sacrament, although in the past and up to Vatican II, the Bible has not been as prominent in the life of the church as in the Protestant churches. It is perhaps distinctive in the way it is governed. Its spiritual leader, the pope, plays a very prominent, some would say dominant, role in the church and has jurisdictional powers over all dioceses in the world.

In spite of the above, the Roman Catholic Church is not as monolithic as some think. For example, there are four main streams of traditions within the Roman Catholic Church, each with one or more 'rites' of its own. Rites basically refer to the style of life of a Christian community. It means more than merely liturgical customs. It is a very comprehensive concept including worship, canon law, asceticism and theological expression. The traditions of the Roman Catholic Church (with their rites given in parenthesis) could be listed as follows: Roman (Latin rite), Antiochene (Armenian, Maronite, Chaldean and Syrian rites), Alexandrian (Coptic rite) and the Byzantine (Melkite, Ukrainian and Russian rites). (Cf. also Appendix D for details on the different rites.)

Facts and figures today

The spread of Protestantism and Anglicanism was rapid. By 1600 most of Germany and Scandinavia were Lutheran; Switzerland, Holland, parts of France, and Scotland were Reformed (in Scotland reformed Christianity was called Presbyterianism), and England was Anglican (cf. map on page 77). With the expansion of the European colonial powers, Christianity in all its manifestations was exported to all corners of the world—North and South America, Africa, Asia and Oceania.

In the USA, the Episcopal Church came into existence. It was not simply a relocation of the Anglican Church from England. The church that was transplanted with the colonists from England reflected the very fluid religious situation in the mother country at the time, and was largely Puritan in nature. What developed in the USA was bound to be something different in character to what was the case in England. As it happened, the first church was built in Jamestown, Virginia, in 1607, but it and subsequent churches were under the jurisdiction of the bishop of London. After the War of Independence, the Protestant Episcopal Church was formally established with its first bishop receiving episcopal ordination in 1784 at the hands of the bishops of the Episcopal Church of Scotland. In 1789 it produced its own revised edition of the *Book of Common Prayer*. It is an autonomous body in full communion with Canterbury. Today it is threatened from within by a conservative subgroup called the Episcopal Synod of America (ESA), which is reacting to the church's perceived liberal trends in such matters as the ordination of women and homosexuals.

In Canada the Anglican Church shares a common origin with the Protestant Episcopalian Church of the USA. In 1787, Charles Inglis, one-time rector of Trinity parish in New York City, was consecrated bishop of Nova Scotia and thus became the first Anglican bishop appointed outside the British Isles. In 1893 a national general synod was established and Canada's first primate elected. Much later, in 1955, the Church of England in Canada changed its name to the Anglican Church of Canada.

The Anglican Church spread to many other parts of the world. In 1814, for example, the first bishop of Calcutta was appointed and not long afterwards bishops in Australia (1836) and New Zealand (1841) followed.

From Germany (and other European countries) the Lutherans made their way to the USA. Their spread and development in the USA from the first church in New York City (1623), is quite complicated in its details. Their development can best be understood if one recalls that, right·from the beginning, there was a multiplicity of Lutheran im-migrants from a variety of European backgrounds, leading to a prolif-eration of Lutheran bodies in the USA. Over the years these smaller churches merged with others in a series of unions. Today there are two main bodies of Lutherans, the New Evangelical Church in America[23] and the Lutheran Church–Missouri Synod[24] noted for its doctrinal conservatism among Lutherans. Taking all Lutheran Churches together, it is the third largest denomination in the USA, after the Roman Catholics and the Baptists.

How have the Reformation churches in general grown numerically over the centuries? The best way to answer that is with the following column graph, which gives contemporary figures for the major Christian churches:[25]

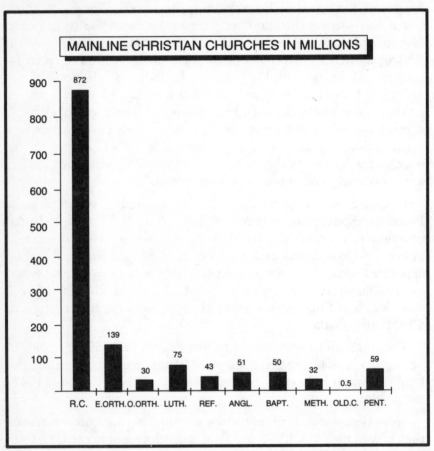

MAINLINE CHRISTIAN CHURCHES IN MILLIONS

	Millions
R.C.	872
E.ORTH.	139
O.ORTH.	30
LUTH.	75
REF.	43
ANGL.	51
BAPT.	50
METH.	32
OLD.C.	0.5
PENT.	59

My aim in the above has not been to give a history of missions (which would require a separate book), but merely to indicate the expansion of the churches of the Reformation era into the New World and link them up with some of the churches we see around us today.

In conclusion it should be noted that on the global scale, although Europe has been the matrix from which Christianity (characterized as predominantly European, white and from the Northern Hemisphere) came to the New World, it is no longer a "European" religion.

Predictions are that, by the next century, the majority of Christians—Protestant and Catholic—will be from the "South", i.e., from the Third World Countries (non-European, dark, and from the Southern hemisphere) as the column graph below shows:[26]

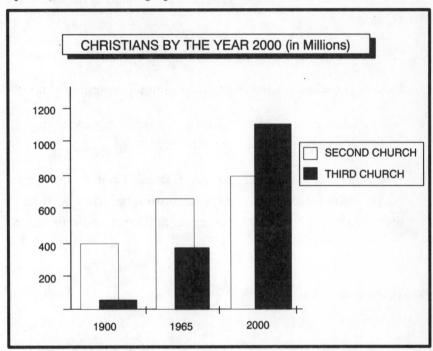

CHRISTIANS BY THE YEAR 2000 (in Millions)

☐ SECOND CHURCH
■ THIRD CHURCH

1200
1000
800
600
400
200

1900   1965   2000

Finally one may ask: What has become of the followers of the Reformers of the sixteenth century? They have all survived time, some have flourished, and new churches have arisen from within the ranks of the Reformation churches, such as the Baptists, Methodists and many more smaller churches (cf. chart on page 28). In other cases, these churches are moving together again in mergers and unions, as we noted in Chapter Two, and by way of the interchurch dialogues, which we will trace further in Chapter Six. The great fragmentation of Christianity that had occurred in the sixteenth and subsequent centuries now seems to be well and truly in reverse gear. The wave of ecumenism that is sweeping the world this century is bringing Christian churches back together. The wounds of the past are being healed.

* * *

Discussion questions

1. What reforms are needed in your church today? Are there any similarities between the need for reform now and in the days of Luther?

2. Do you feel any sympathy for the reformers? Why or why not?

3. In what sense is the Church of England not a Protestant church?

4. What aspects of the Christian faith do you admire most in the Christian churches that you know best?

5. It is sometimes said that the Roman Catholic Church represents "unity without freedom" and Protestantism, "freedom without unity". Give your reasons for agreeing or disagreeing with this opinion.

For further reading:

The Reformation

Chadwick, O., *The Reformation*, Harmondsworth, Pengiun, 1964.

Dickens, A. G., *Reformation and Society*, London, Thames and Hudson, 1966.

—— *The Counter Reformation*, London, Thames and Hudson, 1968.

Delumeau, J., *Catholicism Between Luther and Voltaire*, London, Burns and Oates, 1977.

Elton, G. (ed.), *The Reformation 1520–1559*, New Cambridge Modern History, CUP, 1958.

Grimm, H., *The Reformation Era 1500–1650*, London, Macmillan, 1973.

Hilderbrand, H., *The Reformation*, Grand Rapids, Baker, 1978.

——*Christendom Divided*, New York, Corpus, 1971.

Lortz, J., *How the Reformation Came*, New York, Herder & Herder, 1964.

Rupp, E., *Just Men*, London, Epworth Press, 1977.

Todd, J., *Reformation*, London, DLT, 1971.

Luther

Bainton, R., *Here I Stand*, New York, Abingdon–Cokesbury Press, 1950, and Sutherland, Albatross, 1987.

Brecht, M., *Martin Luther, His Road to Reformation: 1483-1521*, Vol. 1, trans. by J. Schaaf, Minneapolis, Fortress Press, 1985.

—— *Martin Luther, Shaping and Defining the Reformation, 1521-1532*, Vol. 2, trans. by J. Schaaf, Minneapolis, Fortress Press, 1990.

Chadwick, O., *The Reformation*, Harmondsworth, Penguin, 1964.

Clayton, J., *Luther and His Work*, Milwaukee, Bruce, 1937.

Dillenberger, J., *Martin Luther: Selections from His Writings*, New York, Doubleday, 1961.

Ebeling, G., *Luther*, London, Collins, 1970.

Edwards, M., *Luther's Last Battles*, Leiden, Brill, 1983.

Haile, H.G., *Luther: A Biography*, London, Sheldon, 1980.

Oberman, H.A., *Luther: Man Between God and the Devil*, New Haven, Yale UP, 1989.

Oliver, D., *The Trial of Luther*, London, Mowbray, 1971.

Rupp, E., *Martin Luther*, London, Arnold, 1970.

Rupp, E. (ed.), *Luther and Erasmus: Free Will and Salvation*, Philadelphia, Westminster Press, 1969.

Wicks, J., *Luther and His Spiritual Legacy*, Dublin, Dominican Publications, 1983.

Calvin

Bouwsma, W.J., *John Calvin: A Sixteenth Century Portrait*, New York, OUP, 1988.

Graham, W.F., *The Constructive Revolutionary: John Calvin and His Socio-Economic Impact*, Richmond, John Knox Press, 1971.

McNeill, J.T., *The History and Character of Calvinism*, revised edition, New York, OUP, 1966.

McGrath, A., *A Life of John Calvin*, London, Blackwell, 1990.

Parker, T., *John Calvin: A Biography*, London, Dent, 1975.

Richard, L., *The Spirituality of John Calvin*, Atlanta, John Knox Press, 1974.

Walker, W., *John Calvin*, New York, AMS Press, 1972.

Wendel, F., *Calvin*, London, Collins, 1963.

Zwingli

Gäbler, U., *Huldrych Zwingli: His Life and Work*, Philadelphia, Fortress Press, 1986.

Potter, G., *Zwingli*, Cambridge, CUP, 1976.

Stephen, W., *The Theology of Huldrych Zwingli*, Oxford, Clarendon Press, 1986.

Henry VIII

Collinson, P., *The Elizabethan Puritan Movement*, London, Cape, 1967.

—— *The Religion of Protestants: The Church in English Society, 1559–1620*, Oxford, Clarendon Press, 1982.

—— *Godly People: Essays on English Protestantism and Puritanism*, London, Hambledon Press, c. 1983.

Dickens, A.G., *The English Reformation*, revised edition, London, Collins, 1967.

Scarisbrick, J., *Henry VIII*, London, Eyre and Spottiswoode, 1968.

Roman Catholicism

Bishops of the Netherlands, *A New Catechism: Catholic Faith for Adults*, London, Burns and Oates, 1965.

Cunningham, L. (ed.), *The Catholic Faith: A Reader*, New York, Paulist Press, 1988.

McBrien, R., *Catholicism*, Minneapolis, Winston Press, 1980, and Vols I and II, Melbourne, Dove Communications, 1981.

Notes

1. O. Chadwick, *The Reformation*, Harmondsworth, Penguin, 1964, p. 14.
2. *Cambridge Modern History*, 1907, p. 659, cited by W. Durant, *The Story of Civilization VI: The Reformation*, New York, Simon and Schuster, 1957, p. 19.
3. J. Delumeau, *Catholicism Between Luther and Voltaire*, London, Burns and Oates, 1977, p. 157.
4. G. Coulton, *Five Centuries of Religion*, Vol. I: p. 410f, Vol. II: p. 429, cited by Durant, op. cit., p. 20.
5. L. Pastor, *History of the Popes, V*, p. 457f, 1898, cited by Durant, op. cit., p. 21.
6. G. Potter, *Zwingli*, Cambridge, CUP, 1976, p. 11.
7. B. Gascoigne, *The Christians*, London, Jonathan Cape, 1977, p. 144.
8. Delumeau, op. cit., p. 156.
9. H. Lehmann, (ed.), *Luther's Works*, Vol. 44, Philadelphia, Fortress Press, 1966, p. 151.
10. Lehmann, op. cit., Vol. 48, 1963, pp. 45-9.

11. Potter, op. cit., p. 67.
12. J. Todd, *Reformation*, London, DLT, 1971, p. 133.
13. Durant, op. cit., p. 531.
14. Potter, op. cit., p. 112.
15. Chadwick, op. cit., pp. 27–8.
16. Ibid., p. 23.
17. Lehmann, op. cit., Vol. 44, pp. 139–40.
18. Potter, op. cit., p. 114.
19. Chadwick, op. cit., p. 20.
20. H. Grimm, *The Reformation Era 1500–1650*, London, Macmillan, 1973, p. 48.
21. Cited by P. Johnson, *A History of Christianity*, London, Weidenfeld and Nicholson, 1977, p. 278.
22. J. Scarisbrick, *Henry VIII*, London, Eyre and Spottiswoode, 1968, p. 526.
23. The New Evangelical Lutheran Church in America was formed in 1988. This in turn came from two previous groups. (a) The Lutheran Church in America (LCA), the history of which is as follows: In 1918 a number of Lutheran communities formed the United Lutheran Church. This latter church, the ULC, merged with the Swedish-speaking Augustana Lutheran Church (founded in 1860), the Finnish Evangelical Lutheran Church (1890), and the American Evangelical Church (1872), to form the Lutheran Church in America (LCA) in 1962. This latter body was the largest Lutheran denomination in the USA at the time. (b) The second group was the American Lutheran Church established in 1960, like the others, by a merger of existing churches. They were the American Lutheran Church (Germans), the United Evangelical Lutheran Church (Danes) and the Evangelical Lutheran Church (Norwegians), and later joined, in 1963, by the Lutheran Free Church (Norwegian).
24. It has its origins in the church called the German Evangelical Synod of Missouri, Ohio, and Other States, founded by German immigrants from Saxony in 1847.
25. D. Barrett, *World Christian Encyclopedia*, Oxford, OUP, 1982. Individual, more up-to-date figures are available from different sources, e.g., 906 million Roman Catholics for 1991 (*The Tablet*, 28 September 1989). N. Lossky, et al., *Dictionary of the Ecumenical Movement*, Geneva, WCC, 1991, gives statistics for most, but not all churches. Comparisons where possible, are as follows, with Lossky's figures (in millions) in brackets: Eastern Orthodox, 139 (90); Lutheran 75 (59); Reformed 43 (70); Anglican 51 (60); Baptist 50 (65); Methodists 32 (55). Some discrepancies can be explained by the fact that there are different ways of identifying adherents to churches.
26. Figures taken from W. Buhlmann, *The Coming of the Third Church*, Slough, St Paul Publications, 1974, p. 20.

CHAPTER FIVE

Some Contemporary Issues

At the General Assembly of the World Council of Churches in Canberra in 1991, a demonstration with banners and handouts against the assembly was held by a group called "The True Orthodox Christians". It was basically trying to discredit the ecumenical movement and warn people against it. It claimed that ecumenism is faithlessness because it practises a partial faith; it denies the visible existence of the One Church; it is dominated by the spirit of the world; and worse still, it leads to a super-religion which will be the means of the coming reign of the antichrist.[1]

Others too have discredited ecumenism by suggesting it is one big insidious Roman plot to bring all Christians under the power of the papacy once again. The language used in this kind of argumentation is often very emotive and dramatic, and it is still with us. Another argument against ecumenism, used by more conservative people from all churches, is that ecumenism is to be avoided as it waters down the Christian faith in looking for common ground; it is a kind of betrayal of at least some of your religion in order to be nice to others.

However, as more and more people search their hearts, the scandal of disunity becomes more apparent and the above attempts at discrediting ecumenism are seen for what they are—desperate attempts by extreme groups to stop the unstoppable. The rigid positions of these groups has, I believe, resulted in their missing the ecumenical bus. The real ecumenical issues are to be found elsewhere.

Issues of significance come to light when one looks at current dialogues and ecumenical conversations. Let me mention a few and then go into some in greater detail.

Baptism is one issue which seems to have given less trouble in dialogues, resulting in many Christian churches now agreeing to recognize each other's baptisms, although the question of adult or infant baptism remains unresolved between some churches.

On the other hand, the eucharist, which has been the topic of many dialogues, has proved to be more difficult to resolve. This is not really surprising, as it was a bone of contention even among the reformers themselves in the sixteenth century. Related to this is the question of the recognition of ministries. The Roman Catholics, for example, do not recognize the validity of the ordained ministry in the Anglican community, and the Anglicans do not recognize the ministry of non-episcopal churches. Among other churches there are instances where they have recognized each other's ministries, for example, the Methodists, United and Reformed churches in Scotland.

Associated with this is the problem of recognizing marriages contracted in other churches and the problem of how to celebrate a marriage between two people belonging to different Christian churches. These used to be called "mixed marriages" by Roman Catholics and others, and are now called "ecumenical" or "interchurch" marriages. Although the Roman Catholic Church used to look down on these marriages (where one partner was a Roman Catholic) as shameful prior to Vatican II, it now celebrates them with due respect. It continues to insist that the Roman Catholic partner must promise to do all in his or her power to bring up the children as Roman Catholics. The Orthodox insist that if one partner is Orthodox, that they marry in the Orthodox Church and that the Orthodox partner promise to bring up the children as Orthodox. The Reformation churches have been more flexible in these matters and nowadays it is common for two ministers to officiate at an "ecumenical" marriage. Although many problems remain, at least a start has been made to lessen the tensions that such marriages occasioned in the past.

A topic that Roman Catholics thought would be a big obstacle to unity is that of Mariology: the study of Mary and her place in salvation. So far, however, not many dialogues have touched upon this topic which in a way is saying that, in the hierarchy of truths about Christianity, there are other more pressing issues to address first.[2]

A number of discussions have also come to the realization that they need to tackle the ecclesiological question which seems to be at the basis of many of their differences. Whatever their starting point, many dialogues come back to this question of Church sooner or later. The implication here is clear: the nature, mission and structure of the Church is crucial to further ecumenical talks. This includes the thorny issue of authority and supervisory roles in the Church.

One of the most eye-catching and emotive issues is the ordination of women. This issue is often reported on in the press and on television. One reason for its popularity is that it links up with the feminist movement and is part of the broader questions about the position of women regarding education and training, health and child bearing, politics and public life, home and family, and work and money. Let us start with this issue.

Women priests?

There is no doubt that in certain industrialized countries, among certain people, the question of the role of women in ministries, particularly the ordination of women, is a hotly debated issue.

The World Council of Churches' *Baptism, Eucharist and Ministry* document mentions the issue in the context of the call of the whole people of God, without however going into biblical or historical detail regarding the role of women in the early Church.

In recent times some churches have admitted women to various ministries, including that of the ordained ministry. Worldwide, the Anglican communion has consecrated two women bishops, ordained 1342 women and 1942 women deacons, according to a recent tally. The Uniting Church in Australia (formed in 1977 from the Methodist, Congregational and Presbyterian Churches in Australia) has adopted the ordination of women as policy. The Presbyterian Church in Australia (that section that did not join in the union that became the Uniting Church) at first agreed to ordain women and then at a synod in 1991 rescinded its decision, leaving a number of ordained women ministers in a ministerial limbo, so to speak.

Where do other churches stand officially on the question of the ordination of women? The answer can be seen by looking at the response of various churches to the *Baptism, Eucharist and Ministry* document. The document outlines the fact that various churches ordain women and others do not, each for its own reasons. It recognizes that this creates difficulties. Finally the document says, "But those obstacles must not be regarded as substantive hindrance for further efforts towards mutual recognition" (#54). Supporters for the ordination of women are outraged that the issue is thus glossed over. Many negative comments on this point were made about the document. It was called "gravely deficient", "regretfully equivocal" and "evasive and unhelpful". This was seen in the light of the fact that episcopal succession was directly and positively addressed in the same document.

The churches that spoke in favour of the ordination of women included the United Methodist Church in the United Kingdom and in the United States, the Evangelical Methodist Church in Germany, the Church of Christ in Thailand, the Evangelical Presbyterian Church in Ghana (a matriarchal society), the Uniting Church in Australia and the National Council of Churches of Korea. Those against the ordination of women included the Roman Catholic Church,[3] and the Orthodox churches in general throughout the world. Some churches were divided, like the Anglicans from one diocese to the next throughout the world, and the Scottish Episcopal Church. Others were divided from one country to the next, for example, the Lutheran Church (Missouri Synod) was in favour, while the Lutherans in Australia were against. Likewise, the Presbyterians in the United States are for, while those in Australia recently changed their minds and are now against, as mentioned above.

What are the reasons that are being put forward by each side? To put it briefly, the Anglicans argue that there are positive theological reasons for why women should be ordained. It is not merely a question of there being no objections to it. Firstly, Galatians 3:28 is taken seriously in saying that the male-female, along with all social barriers, have been removed for Christians, who now share a radical equality. They argue too that the humanity taken on by the Word must be a humanity inclusive of women. The ministerial priesthood represents the priestly nature of the whole body of the Church and stands in a special sacramental relationship with Christ as High Priest in whom complete humanity is redeemed. Because the humanity of Christ includes male and female, the ministerial priesthood should be opened to women in order to represent more perfectly Christ's inclusive High Priesthood. In addition to these theological reasons, Anglicans also cite their own beneficial experience where women have already been ordained.

"I fear those are indeed our Roman Catholic opposite numbers . . ."

"I'm all for Ecumenism . . . but would somebody please disengage us!"

On the other side, Roman Catholics argue strongly that they are not empowered to change a 2,000-year-old tradition of males only. In addition they put forward Christological arguments. They maintain that the ministerial priest stands *in persona Christi*, with the emphasis on him firstly representing Christ rather than on representing the whole People of God. Christ came as a man and his male identity is seen as an inherent feature of the economy of salvation. This gives the sacramental ordination of men added force and significance within the context of salvation. It can be seen that whereas the Anglicans emphasize that Christ assumed humanity, the Roman Catholic argument stresses that he assumed maleness within that humanity.

The Bible has often been used in this debate. The Orthodox have categorically said that ordination is only for males according to the Bible and tradition, quoting the example of Christ and the Apostles, all of whom were male. Other churches, for example, the Lutherans, are less certain. Part of their church uses biblical data to support the ordination of women while others use the same Bible to support the case against it!

With the Orthodox and the Roman Catholics, the emphasis is also on seeing the ordained ministry as a sacrament. Those that argue for the ordination of women tend to see it more as a function. This does not necessarily mean that they deny it is a sacrament. It is a question of emphasis. The Anglicans, for example, do not deny that the ordained ministry is a sacrament, but argue for the ordination of women. Those that place emphasis on the ordained ministry as a function tend to see the question as one of church discipline rather than doctrine. Those that see it as a sacrament tend to argue that the question of the ordination of women is a doctrinal one. Needless to say, the issue remains unresolved among the churches.

It is important that where differences exist the parties keep talking. It is therefore disturbing to find the attitude that was expressed by one Orthodox Church representative who referred to the issue as "a matter which in our church was made clear long ago". This attitude seems to reject totally the statement of *Baptism, Eucharist and Ministry*, that "Openness to each other holds the possibility that the Spirit may well speak to one church through the insights of another" (#54). How can the churches learn from the Holy Spirit through listening to each other if the issues are finalized before they dialogue? The spirit and the theology of ecumenism, as we saw in Chapter One, implies a search for truth and being led by the Holy Spirit, perhaps into areas unfamiliar to the churches.

The above opinions reflect the official position of churches, but we all know that within even conservative churches like the Roman Catholic Church, dissident voices can be heard. One can certainly say that among the more conservative churches the tendency is against women's ordination, and less so among the Free or Independent churches. That is only one way to categorize the issue. Within churches one finds a broad spectrum of opinions from the extreme right to the extreme left, some depending on how fundamentalistically the Bible is interpreted, others on whether tradition is perceived as something dynamic or set in concrete. This would certainly apply to the Orthodox and Roman Catholic Churches, especially evident in the latter after Vatican II.

Let me illustrate from another example. The Presbyterian Church in Australia was divided over the issue of unification with the Congregationalists and Methodists in 1977. It was the conservative wing, by and large, that stayed out of the union. Why? Perhaps because a conservative approach tends to carry over into many issues. Perhaps those, in whatever church, who are in favour of the ordination of women, are those that tend to be progressive, open to change, willing to experiment, willing to read the gospels and tradition again without preconceived ideas. Likewise those who reject the ordination of women, tend to be those who are doctrinally conservative, closed to new ideas, unwilling to change.

One factor that does influence the debate and will continue to do so, is the sociological fact that the role of women in society has changed in recent decades. Particularly in industrialized society today, women have stepped into roles in politics, business and government that have been traditionally the preserve of males. This movement has influenced the churches, even if some would not admit to it.

Let me give an example. The Roman Catholic Church has spoken out against the ordination of women, yet at the same time over the last twenty-five years, girls have appeared here and there as altar servers, women have taken on the role of lectors and as special ministers of the eucharist, that is, distributing communion. In addition to all this, it is well known that nuns, having reconsidered their mission in many cases, have here and there emerged as parish pastoral associates or a similar title, that is, assistants to the parish priest. This often means taking on almost all the ministries in the parish except celebrating the eucharist and administering absolution. The anomaly is that this contribution goes by largely unacknowledged for what it is—a woman being virtually an assistant parish priest. The evolution of the role of women in society has made this possible and will continue to put pressure on those churches who do not currently ordain women. Not that sociology will bend the theological arguments, but that it will help some theologians apply the hermeneutic of suspicion to their cherished theological arguments.

One can also challenge the arguments used from the consequences of the ordination of women. Among the Anglican community it has been said that it has divided people and dioceses, caused tensions between bishops, caused all kinds of legal challenges. On an ecumenical level the pope and others have repeatedly maintained that the ordination of women is an obstacle to further progress between the churches. All these are arguments against the ordination of women.

The contrary point of view has also to be considered, namely, what are the consequences if the churches continue to refuse ordination to women, and the broader question of refusing them a rightful place in church ministry contrary to the New Testament church? In dioceses where women are not ordained, it has caused great frustration among some women. How can churches continue to deny ministries to a group of persons who make up well over half of its practising members? The National Council of Korea claims that 70% of its congregations are women. Do the churches run the risk of causing a schism if they do *not* ordain women? Who will be left in the mainline churches if all the women leave?

The sociological argument needs to be approached with caution as there are other societies where, for cultural reasons, the role of women is not undergoing the same changes as in western society. There are also matriarchal societies, as in Ghana, where the argument simply does not apply. All this leads some to conclude that the issue of whether women should be ordained might best be determined by the local church. They see no reason why all churches have to practise the same church discipline in this matter, and indeed they see strong cultural reasons why they should not. Looking to a future united church, some think of a unity in creeds and doctrine, but to a pluralism in church practices and theologies not too dissimilar to the New Testament churches.

Let us return to the *Baptism, Eucharist and Ministry* document, because this text places the debate about the ordination of women in its rightful context of ministry in general. The larger context includes the questions of what is ministry? Who can minister? What is the best way to use the gifts of the Spirit present in church members? What exactly is the role of one who presides over the eucharist? How is authority to be used in coordinating ministries? And perhaps underlying them all, What understanding of Church speaks best to us today in this society? One's answer to the question about the ordination of women has really got to be given with answers to all these other related questions. As was remarked earlier, sooner or later we come back to ecclesiological questions.

The eucharist

There are different meanings we give to this word, eucharist. Firstly, there is the eucharist in the sense of the entire religious ceremony (eucharistic celebration or Mass) as a whole and its meaning, and secondly, the eucharist in the sense of the bread and wine as partaking in the Lord's Supper or Holy Communion.

With the first meaning, the questions that are often posed relate to the meaning of the eucharist. Is it a prayer of thanksgiving only? Is it also a sacrifice? If so, in what way is it a sacrifice? As regards the second meaning of the eucharist, the questions often focus on the meaning of the Real Presence: in what way is Christ present? What does transubstantiation mean? What happens to the bread and wine? Does one have to believe, in order for Christ to be present?

So it is not surprising that *The Final Report*[4] addresses these issues. Firstly, let us discuss the eucharist in the first sense mentioned above. One will quickly note that the document does not so much present a theology of the eucharist as make a number of doctrinal statements. It begins its statement by speaking about the mystery of the eucharist. It sees the eucharist as the saving act of our redemption. In it Christ makes effective among us the eternal benefit of his victory. Through it, Christ, through the Holy Spirit, builds up the Church, strengthens its fellowship and furthers its mission. It is eschatological, it proclaims his death until he comes.

Is the eucharist a sacrifice? The document is at pains to stress that Calvary was a once-only event. Any attempt to make a nexus between Calvary and the eucharist must bear this in mind. *The Final Report* chooses to make use of the term *memorial (anamnesis)* to make the link between the sacrifice of Christ and the eucharist. But the meaning of "memorial" is technical. It is used as in the time of Christ, in the context of the celebration of the passover. *It is the making effective in the present an event which happened in the past.* So the eucharistic memorial is no mere calling to mind of something that happened in the past, it is no mere empty recollection of a memory. It is the making effective in the present of something that occurred in the past.

Sacrament and Sacrifice,[5] the result of the dialogue between Roman Catholics and Lutherans in Australia, approaches the topic in a different way. As a general statement, it says that Christ's death on Calvary was the sacrifice for the sins of the whole world, and refers to the eucharist as "a sacrifice of praise and thanksgiving". It is left to Section V to deal with the specific differences between Lutherans and Catholics on this issue of the eucharist as a sacrifice.

From a Protestant point of view, safeguards have to be given that each eucharist/Mass is not seen as a repeat of Calvary. Lutherans have often assumed that Catholics were saying precisely this. Bearing this in mind, *Sacrament and Sacrifice* stresses that both parties agree that Calvary as a sacrifice is "unique, unrepeatable, and complete". Having settled that issue, the focus moves to Christians' participation in the sacrificial death of Christ in the eucharist. Here the question is thus not *whether* believers participate in Christ's sacrificial death in the eucharist, but *how* this participation is to be understood.

The Catholic position can be expressed thus: they believe that because of their baptismal union with Christ, they are drawn in the eucharist into Christ's self-offering to the Father in such a way that they become participants in Christ's offering of himself. Lutherans, on the other hand, stress God's forgiveness to the faithful communicated in the eucharist. The faithful receive what Christ has won for them on the cross. Because of this emphasis, Lutherans steer clear of any suggestion that Christ, or his sacrifice on the cross, is offered up by the faithful, by the priest, or by the Church. This discussion of different emphases by the two traditions, has raised for Catholics the role of the eucharist in the forgiveness of sins—a role that has been there in the background but largely neglected.

How does the *Baptism, Eucharist and Ministry* document deal with these problems? It sees the eucharist as an act of thanksgiving to the Father and then also invokes the concept of *anamnesis* or memorial, i.e., "the living and effective sign of his sacrifice, accomplished once and for all on the cross and still operative on behalf of all humankind".[6]

The authors of this document were well aware of the history of controversy surrounding the use of "sacrifice" in connection with the eucharist, so it invites all churches to re-examine the word and especially in the ecumenical climate of open-mindedness, to see if they can at least grasp why some have used the term and others made a point of avoiding it.[7]

The Real Presence

The second sense in which the eucharist is used is that of Holy Communion or partaking of the Lord's Supper. It is addressed by the same three documents mentioned above.

The Final Report says there has been substantial agreement consistent with a variety of theological approaches within both communions, that is, the Roman Catholic and Anglican communions. The document mentions the Real Presence of Christ. The fact is simply affirmed. It then goes on to mention that traditionally contentious word "transubstantiation". It notes that contemporary Roman Catholic theology sees the word "transubstantiation" as affirming the presence of Christ, not explaining *how* Christ is present. It also makes the point that the Real Presence is not dependent on the individual's faith.

When speaking of the Real Presence, *The Final Report* uses the terminology of "becoming" and "changing" which in a way invites the question of how this becoming and change occurs. The response to the document picked this up and criticised the document accordingly.

Sacrament and Sacrifice speaks of the Real Presence as being grasped by faith (not dependent on faith). The document grapples with the notion of Real Presence, trying to say what it is, and what it is not. It is the physical presence of the Risen Christ; but not "physical" understood in a crass sort of way. It states that it is certainly more than a moral presence. It is a special kind of presence, called a "sacramental presence", but in no way inferior to the presence of the earthly Christ to his disciples. This is probably more helpful in what it rules out than in what it asserts.

The document says that Lutherans and Catholics have both held firmly to their belief in Christ's real presence in the eucharist. Differences have appeared in the various ways each has tried to safeguard this belief. Lutherans have used the analogy of the hypostatic union of the divine and human natures in Christ to speak about the fact that the bread and wine and Christ's body and blood are one with each other in the eucharist. Catholics instead have spoken about the same fact in the Aristotelian-Scholastic terms of the 'substance' of the bread and wine being changed into the 'substance' of the body and blood of Christ while the 'accidents' of bread and wine remain. (This whole debate needs to be updated in the light of quantum physics which has drastically changed the Newtonian understanding of the material world. Recourse to an outmoded ontology of substance and accidents is no longer acceptable. New ways of speaking not only of the eucharist, but also of the Incarnation and Resurrection will have to be explored.[8])

The document has a useful appendix on the history and use of the term 'transubstantiation'. It concludes by saying that Catholics remain loyal to Trent if they continue to affirm the Real Presence irrespective of whether they choose to use the term transubstantiation. So the question of how this Real Presence occurs is not really explained. Saying it is a sacramental presence does not really satisfy, but then what language will?

The *Baptism, Eucharist and Ministry* document also confronts the question of the Real Presence. It speaks about the eucharist as the sacrament of his real presence (#13). It is a unique mode of Christ's presence. It speaks about "Christ's real, living and active presence in the eucharist". Like the *Sacrament and Sacrifice* document, it says that this presence does not depend on the faith of the individual, yet everyone agrees that to discern Christ's presence requires faith.

In the commentary on #13, it mentions a problem that some churches have—they do not link real presence with signs of bread and wine so definitely. It invites them to decide if the text, as it is, can accommodate them. There is an obvious problem here with a text that is trying to satisfy so many different theologies of the Real Presence, especially those, such as the Reformed churches, which tend towards the symbolic understanding rather than emphasize its reality. One is reminded here of the fact that the churches which participated in the document ranged right across the Christian spectrum from the Roman Catholic and Orthodox to Adventists and Pentecostals. So it is not surprising that the document lacks the tightness of the two previous statements.

Intercommunion

By intercommunion is meant the reception of the consecrated eucharistic bread and wine by Christians at services in churches other than their own. The Latin expression used is *communicatio in sacris*, communion in sacred things. The Orthodox and Roman Catholic churches do not generally allow this, but other churches often do.

The first issue to consider here is what different churches believe about eucharistic communion. Even though the Orthodox and Roman Catholic churches have a common understanding of the eucharist, they do not have the same rules about receiving it. Roman Catholics allow Orthodox to receive the eucharist in their churches but the reverse is not the case, except in cases of extreme urgency. The Orthodox, moreover, discourage their own faithful from receiving in Roman Catholic churches. There would be less similarity between other churches, so the question then is: does the other church believe the same about this eucharistic communion as we do? Churches are understandably reluctant to allow people to their communion table if they know they do not share their beliefs about the eucharist. On the other hand, there is often more difference about what a given church tradition believes about the eucharist *within* that tradition than *between* one tradition and another.

The second issue regards the significance of eucharistic communion. The eucharist is central to the religious lives of many Christians and, not surprisingly, is closely connected with descriptions of the nature of the Church. This nexus is brought home in many different ways and places. Let me give two examples which show two different approaches to the issue. In 1992, Italian Baptist and Lutheran leaders boycotted the Mass for the Week of Prayer for Christian Unity (25 January) in Rome, because they were excluded from full participation by not being allowed to take communion. Secondly, at the recent Seventh Assembly of the World Council of Churches in Canberra (1991), the Orthodox produced a statement after the conclusion of business, raising some problems they had with the assembly, as mentioned in Chapter Two. One of these problems concerned the eucharist and ecclesiology. At the end of the assembly there was the common Lima liturgy in which all were expected to participate. The Orthodox however did not receive eucharistic communion at this common worship and as a result drew criticism upon themselves. It appeared to some critics that their attitude was somewhat triumphalistic.[9]

The Orthodox, in response, pointed out that this was not the case, but that their stance related to their understanding of ecclesiology which saw eucharistic communion as only possible when complete ecclesiological unity had been achieved. For them, eucharistic communion is an expression of ecclesiological unity, not a means to that end. Roman Catholics have also expressed the same position. So, one way or another, the underlying issue of ecclesiology must be addressed if ecumenical conversations are going to progress towards reunion.

This incident highlights the crux of the matter. For some churches (Orthodox, Roman Catholic) the reception of eucharistic communion is primarily a sign or expression of full unity, whereas for other churches it is primarily a means of grace, and thus for furthering unity. The Roman Catholic Church has, since Vatican II, published a number of documents all disapproving of intercommunion except in cases of great urgency.[10] A case of urgency would be someone who, on a permanent basis, did not have a minister of his or her own denomination available.

Quite a different approach is taken by those who take the sacrament of baptism as the basis for receiving communion. For example, the Ukrainians (and others) believe that once baptised, one is a full member of a church and, as such, entitled to receive the eucharist. Thus they give infants Holy Communion. Now if one accepts this point of view and if one recognizes baptism as valid in another church, then logically why not allow intercommunion with that church?

The problem is a vexed one and is far from being resolved among the churches.

Membership of the Church

We mentioned that many dialogues have come to realize that the topic of Church[11] itself must be confronted sooner or later. There are of course many aspects to this large topic, such as nature, mission, structure, authority, etc. We will consider first the question of membership of the Church, as it has already received some attention in debates. Let us examine the case of the Roman Catholic concept of Church.

Prior to Vatican II, the Roman Catholics in *Mystici Corporis* (1943) and *Humani Generis* (1950), both by Pius XII, made it clear that the Mystical Body of Christ, the Church of Christ, and the Roman Catholic Church are one and the same thing. The Second Vatican Council qualified this in a very significant way. Some might say the Catholic Church did a U-turn on this issue, but history shows that western tradition has implicitly entertained the certainty that the Church of God extends beyond the limits of the churches in communion with the see of Rome. The Council of Florence in 1439, for example, accepted that the Church had been divided into two parts. Yves Congar speaks about the two lungs of the Church, the East and West.

The Vatican II Preparatory Commission in 1962 took the traditional line on this matter. It wrote: "The Roman Catholic Church is the Mystical Body of Christ ... and only the one that is Roman Catholic has the right to be called Church".[12] A new schema in 1963 added the following words when speaking about the Church: "... many elements of sanctification can be found outside its total structure and that these are things properly belonging to the Church of Christ". In 1964 the commission reflected on this addition and raised the question of the inconsistency in speaking about elements outside the structure and the simple statement of equating the Roman Catholic Church with the Church of Christ.

The solution was suggested by the Council Fathers in the simple replacement of "is" with "subsists in". The Church of Christ "subsists in" the Catholic Church. The reason for this change was given in the explanation: "so that the expression might better agree with the affirmation about the ecclesial elements which are found elsewhere".[13] The Council Fathers seemed to have reasoned that whoever belongs to Christ belongs to the Church, and hence that the limits of the Church are coextensive with those belonging to Christ. This, according to Willebrands, was the dogmatic reflection behind the transition from *est* to *subsistit in*.[14]

The document *Lumen Gentium* (Dogmatic Constitution on the Church) was recommended to be interpreted in the light of the *Decree on Ecumenism*, and they were published on the same day. Commentators are agreed that this change of wording heralds a significant opening towards the recognition of ecclesial reality in the Christian world which is other than Roman Catholic.

Church as *koinonia*

One of the obvious images of church that is emerging in our times is that of Church as *koinonia*,[15] as we saw in some detail in Chapter One. The ARCIC II committee has published a report with the title of *The Church as Communion*. ARCIC I also mentioned *koinonia* as did the Vatican II documents. It is also part of the tradition of the Orthodox Church to see the Church as *koinonia*. However, there are many models of Church, each with its own validity.

Let me briefly reiterate what was said in Chapter One. The question is, which model of Church most appeals to people at a particular time in history. At the moment people are moving away from some models of Church (especially the hierarchical one which has been overplayed in some churches), and favouring the *koinonia* model which stresses what we have in common, what we share as God's children redeemed by Christ. "*Koinonia*, whether between God and humanity or among human beings, must be regarded as a gift from God", says the Baptist-Roman Catholic report (#21).

Each church since the Reformation has kept and preserved some elements of Christianity better than others. We can learn from all churches. The Reformed churches have preserved great respect and devotion to the Word of God in the Bible and in preaching, Methodists in involvement in social justice issues, the Orthodox in preserving the mystagogical aspects of the eucharist, and the Baptists in *koinonia*, in the sense of fellowship. There will be other aspects of Christianity to be rediscovered as we progress on the ecumenical journey.

Authority and the Church

This is another topic which must be grappled with if progress is to be made on the ecumenical front. ARCIC I has two agreed statements on authority in the Church. The first (1976) agrees on much as regards *koinonia*, *episcope*, and conciliar and primatial authority. It does, however, have some sticking points for Anglicans. Firstly, Catholics, it is felt, have placed too much weight on the Petrine texts (those passages in the New Testament referring to Peter) in the past in proving their point. Secondly, Vatican I's use of the "divine right" of the successors of Peter would be a problem if it suggested that a church not in communion with Rome would be less than fully a church. Thirdly, there is a problem with the concept and the use of the word 'infallibility'.

In passing it may be useful to point out that others, like the Baptists, have a difficulty of a more fundamental nature, namely that all the structures of the Church are human and so are not wedded to any particular ones.

ARCIC I recognizes, in general terms, the idea of Roman primacy. The specific question is, what is the function and role of that primacy? Archbishop Runcie said that he himself had no problem with the idea of a pope in a future united church, but that the way that role is defined and exercised is crucial. One of the concerns of the Anglicans is that Rome might want to impose the uniformity on a future united church that she (the Catholic Church) has traditionally placed on the local churches of the Latin West.

The problem of the pope's immediate jurisdictional power over every diocese is a problem for the Anglicans, Orthodox and many more. It is by no means a hypothetical issue. A contemporary example, not likely to further the cause of ecumenism, was that of Archbishop Hunthausen of Seattle. The Vatican intervened directly, when after investigations in 1986, it ordered him to turn over authority in several areas to Auxiliary Bishop Donald Wuerl. Even though he was fully restored in 1987, the damage had been done. A year later Hunthausen, in a letter to the Holy See, pointed out that the same painful experiences could occur in other dioceses if the Vatican gave credibility to mean-spirited criticism from a small group of people intent on undermining church unity.

According to the Orthodox, who would oppose this kind of direct intervention, the pope can be called *primus inter pares* (first among equals), and the Lutherans speak of the value of the 'Petrine function'. The Methodists are more cautious. They note that it might be possible to have an agreed perception of what functions the See of Rome might properly exercise in a ministry of universal unity. However, the basis of the authority and the conditions would have to be carefully scrutinized.

The Anglicans, like the Orthodox, have experienced a diversity in their traditions that they are not likely to easily compromise in the future. Indeed the early Church, the Church of the New Testament, was a diverse church in many aspects of its life. The document therefore suggests that Roman Catholics could learn from the Anglicans in the areas of diversity in unity, synodal tradition and involvement of the laity.

In the Roman Church, synods and councils are mainly, or entirely, clerical meetings, whereas in the Anglican Church, lay membership of these decision-making bodies is normal.

The document *Church as Communion* indicates that further study is needed on episcopal authority, particularly of universal primacy, and of the office of the Bishop of Rome; on the question of provincial autonomy in the Anglican communion; and on the role of the laity in decision-making within the Church. These issues have arisen out of the Anglican-Roman Catholic dialogue but they are topics that other churches will have to address as well. Churches are at different stages in their discussions and it would be fair to say that the further apart they were in recent history, the longer it will take to broach some of these very substantive issues.

Baptism, Eucharist and Ministry, which represents a very broad spectrum of churches, does not address the issue to the same extent. It is more interested in ministry as such in the Christian Church. It therefore speaks about the authority of the minister; the authority of Jesus; the authority of the ordained minister and the danger of the distortion of isolation and domination.

Conversion and proselytism

In the Baptist-Roman Catholic conversations some interesting topics arose. These come to the fore in the report of the committee in a document entitled, *Summons to Witness to Christ in Today's World* (1988).

One is the issue of conversion in Christian life. The Baptists have traditionally made a big point about the conversion experience and in doing so they stand in the company of Paul of Tarsus and many other illustrious Christians including Luther and Calvin. Roman Catholics, on the other hand, practising infant baptism, tend to give less importance to a particular experience of conversion in their life of faith. A life of faith could be seen as something that grows steadily from baptism, almost a socialization process. One grows into one's religion. For the Baptists the initial experience of personal *metanoia* is clear, sharp and decisive. Only when one is converted can baptism take place formally.

In a way, Roman Catholics have learnt something from the Baptist tradition when they say in their *Rite for the Christian Initiation of*

Adults (RCIA) that adult baptism is the paradigm for Christian life. The important point here is that individuals need to commit themselves fully and consciously to Christ. Baptists, on the other hand, by not baptising infants are perhaps not considering the importance of the faith of the community into which one is born and that the community can speak for the child in matters of faith until the child can speak for itself.

Both communities can therefore re-examine their understanding of conversion and theology of baptism. This is an ecumenical theology of origins and sources at its best—going back to fundamentals, which is quite different to fundamentalism! This is what the *Decree on Ecumenism* is saying when it invites all to renew themselves as a first step in ecumenism.

Another issue, related to conversion, which has surfaced with some feeling, is that of proselytism. It used to have a good meaning. It referred to someone who had converted from paganism. But in recent times is has come to acquire a perjorative sense, namely the unfair actions of one church to win members from another church. This issue cropped up in the Baptist-Roman Catholic conversations (it gets extensive coverage with thirteen paragraphs of the report devoted to this issue), in the Coptic-Roman Catholic dialogue, the Orthodox-Roman Catholic dialogue and probably in others as well. In the Orthodox-Roman Catholic dialogue, as we saw in the previous chapter, the Orthodox have said that uniatism will be taken as a sign that the Roman Catholics are not serious about ecumenism.

The problem comes back in time and history when in some countries the religious minorities were put under pressure—financial, social, or even physical—to change their religious allegiance. Unfortunately this problem is still with us today in spite of a lot of talk about religious freedom.

Cooperation of ministers/priests

One of the unspoken issues in ecumenism today is that of the cooperation of church ministers in the promotion of ecumenism. Working at the international level this is not an issue at all, since those who have agreed to represent their churches are presumably favourably disposed to ecumenism. But when one tries to do something at the local level, cooperation of ministers/priests is quite a formidable issue.

The issue is that many (not all) ministers or priests do not actively promote and cooperate with each other and other church communities in ecumenical matters and, by not doing so, make it pretty difficult for anyone else to do something.

This might sound strange, but my personal experience and the experience of others confirms this. The following telling excerpt, written by a minister, is still applicable today. It comes from a report by the Secretary of the New South Wales (Australia) State Committee on Local Ecumenism and says it all:

> As a priest of the Church of God I am often saddened
> that the failure of the churches in the local area to
> become engaged in ecumenical action is due not to
> irreconcilable doctrinal or traditional approaches, but
> simply to the personality clashes between brother
> clergy. The office of a pastor in the Church of God
> brings many temptations—to make oneself the pivot
> and kingpin, to claim status for oneself, to become an
> individualist, to make theology or liturgy into the
> minister's mystic preserve, to see and speak of the
> claims of Christ over others and to ignore His demands
> of service, persistence, discipline and obedience
> oneself. We clergy are often the greatest hindrance
> to God and His mission. (*Ecumenical Work*, 1964.)

This is a pretty sobering statement. The last sentence shows the importance and wisdom of going back to basics about Christianity in the pursuit of ecumenism. What is the mission of Christ and his Church and how are we trying to achieve it? It is tragic if those entrusted with being the spiritual leaders in furthering the mission are actually guilty of hindering it. Such unfortunately seems to be the case in many instances.

The importance of getting back to basics was brought home to me recently in a dramatic way. I was attending the installation ceremony of a minister of a Uniting Church community. This was not his first parish by any means. He had had plenty of pastoral experience, yet the ceremony included reminding him of his duties to the parishioners. Two parishioners presented him with a Bible and pointed out to him his duty to proclaim the Word of God; others presented him with bread and wine as a reminder to celebrate the Lord's Supper for them; others, a jug of water and basin for baptism; others again reminded him of his duty of pastoral care of all in the parish. In each case he articulated his readiness to fulfil these duties. I thought it a wholesome ritual for all the community and a dramatic reminder of congregational priorities. In a parish where one incumbent is there for a lifetime, this kind of recommitment on the part of the parish and the minister can be lacking.

For a moment though, let us look at the issue of the cooperation of ministers from a sociological point of view. A minister has a group of people who come together for a particular common purpose. He or she is unlikely to support movements which are seen as threatening the cohesion of that group. If an interchurch group begins to hold Bible study evenings, it might be seen as drawing them away from their own church. (It might also stimulate some churches into forming their own if they don't have any!) Ecumenism could easily be seen as some kind of takeover bid or amalgamation attempt in which smaller groups (individual parishes) might be swallowed up. Politically speaking, the local minister of a congregation has power over the flock and is not going to promote developments that are perceived as potentially threatening to destroy the basis of that power.

Financially too, ministers are keen to maintain the flow of cash from their parishioners to continue funding worthwhile projects like church schools, church buildings and maintenance programs. Ecumenical ventures that might disaffect their financial contributors and cut off their money supply must be seen as a threat.

And to complete the picture, it must be said that within the Roman Catholic Church, at least in certain countries, a heavy burden has been placed on the parish priests. They were trained to be spiritual leaders of their flock, but with time and in practice, the expectation of them is that they should be successful fund-raisers, loan organizers, managers of primary schools and financial advisers to huge regional secondary schools. That some have warmed to the task is no excuse for this unfortunate historical development.

To talk in these terms is not to belittle the faith of Christian churches, but simply to describe the all too human side of the Church, parishioners and ministers.

This issue of the cooperation of ministers in the promotion of ecumenism has, as we have seen, significant sociological, financial and political dimensions. To transcend these the ministers have to be truly spiritual people, committed to Christ's and the Church's mission as those involved in Local Ecumenical Projects (called LEPs) obviously are. Their theology must not be overwhelmed by the ideologies and praxis of power-wielding. No wonder ecumenism demands a change of heart and reconversion to the gospel as a first step! It is valid for the ordinary parishioner. It is equally valid for their spiritual leaders.

Where pastors have engaged in ecumenism they have found it the opposite to what many feared. Instead of being yet another energy-sapping activity to add to an already heavy workload, they have found it marvellously revitalizing as if the process of working with other Christian churches has suddenly released a powerhouse of new life. This should not come as a surprise to Christians who believe in the gospel paradoxes.

Methodology in dialogues

The question of how to conduct dialogues, that is, the methodology implicit in the procedures, has become an explicit issue of the ecumenical movement. Perhaps at the beginning one might have seen it only as a procedural and political dimension to dialogues, but now it has produced some very interesting and unforeseen theological spin-offs.

The Orthodox have said they are not happy with the methodology pursued in arriving at agreed statements. Most dialogues seem to come out with a common or agreed statement at the end of the sessions. Editing committees from both sides work on a statement agreeable to both churches as represented at the dialogues. Then the full committee votes on the text. This text is sometimes spoken of as a convergence text like the Lima Document (*Baptism, Eucharist and Ministry*). The phrase "a convergence text" is a little perjorative in the sense that the need to compromise in wording is thought to have been uppermost in the minds of those doing the writing, rather than in saying what they strongly believed on an issue.

The Orthodox think this method obscures the differences between the parties and thus actually hinders honest dialogue. The *Decree on Ecumenism* warns one against a false irenicism. Now the Orthodox are repeating the warning. They have suggested each side produce its own statement on the topic and then an editing team use these documents to write a convergence statement. In that way both the common points and the differences would get highlighted. With the current method of only producing the agreed statement, the common points eclipse the differences, they think.

With this suggestion one has to remind oneself that the ecumenical movement has relied very heavily on the principle that for years Christians have emphasized their differences, and that they now want to stress what they have in common. The vocabulary of John XXIII typifies this with the switch from "Protestants" to "separated brethren". On the other hand, the Orthodox have a point. If we pretend that there are no serious differences in some cases, we do ecumenism a disservice.

Other than the Orthodox solution, which to me stresses the differences, there is another approach, such as the one used in the *Sacrament and Sacrifice* statement of the Lutheran-Roman Catholic dialogue in Australia. There a common statement is written followed by ample space for each party to explain at some length their own particular theologies, emphases or concerns. I believe that overall this approach is more positive, without losing the importance of a measured articulation of differences. *The Final Report* also follows this methodology with its agreed statements, matters yet to be resolved, and then "Elucidations" which respond to critical comments.

The actual theological way in which these statements are written is another focus of scrutiny. The Roman Catholics, and some other churches, prefer the discursive, scientific, intellectual way of theologizing in the tradition of western rationalism. This has been the traditional way since the scholastic period of handing on a theology (I would not say "doing theology"). The Orthodox, on the other hand, reflecting an eastern approach, would be more at home with less emphasis on the rational and more importance given to the mysterious in matters of faith. The Pentecostals reflect again a quite different approach. They are more at home with oral and narrative theology. They give great emphasis to testimony and spiritual experience as validating truth. They also place great value on the exercise of spiritual gifts and would like theological exchange to take place in this context rather than in the rational, abstract atmosphere of concepts.

Models of unity

Another issue is that of the model of unity which people may have in mind when thinking of a united church of the future. Some think that no one seems to know where it is all heading, rather like being on a speeding train without a driver. This is in fact more or less the case! Some think that Rome has a secret agenda, but more think that the Holy Spirit is inspiring the movement and leading it.

When one begins to discuss ecumenism seriously in a group, sooner or later it becomes apparent that each individual might have different views on what the final goal is. We noted above how the Orthodox churches think the World Council of Churches needs to focus more sharply on where it is going. Some conservative Roman Catholics, as well as the Reverend Paisley, have understood it as a "back-to-Rome" movement, the end goal being the organic unity of smaller churches under the papacy. At the other end of the spectrum are those who see solidarity with the poor as the distinguishing characteristic of the future church, not denominational boundaries.[16] In between one has variations of covenanting, integration and joint councils.

The Jehovah Witnesses' magazine, *Awake*,[17] makes the point that Roman Catholics do not intend to change, so beware of their ecumenical intentions on you! They also raise the question of the true Church and Roman Catholic teaching about that.

I personally like to envisage ecumenism as a *dynamic* movement of all churches forward (thus giving up one's current position, painful though it may be!) to a future organic unity yet to be worked out in detail. The problem with the argument about the Catholic Church claiming to be the one, true Church assumes that churches are static, whereas I am saying that ecumenism is dynamic, that churches involved in ecumenism are dynamic, changing, growing and learning. If they all travel a road together, the road ahead is more important in a sense than their present positions. That is not to say faithfulness to the past is set aside, but rather to ask: How can we be faithful to the past in the future?

In thinking about possible models of future unity it is important not to confuse conformity with unity as was done in the earlier relationship between Rome and Constantinople, as we saw in Chapter Two. The Latin Western (Roman) Church has tended to impose uniformity since the times of the Roman Empire. The Eastern churches, however, quickly established their system of local churches and patriarchates which rejected a centralized system. Since the Reformation, the Protestant churches, too, have tended to reject centralized, interventionist structures.

Actually, as was pointed out in Chapter Four, although the Roman Catholic Church has appeared to be a very monolithic, uniform church, in reality it is not. One could quote many examples, but one will suffice. The Ukrainian rite, for example, has married priests although this was one of the best kept secrets in my religious upbringing, presumably because knowledge thereof might threaten the apparent neat uniformity of the Western Church! Diversity has been there in the past and will be there in a future united church. It is misleading to pretend otherwise.

Along with Congar, I hope that in a future unified Christian church there will be plenty of room for diversity, not only of customs but also of theological expression, while preserving unity. Unfortunately the Roman Catholic Church for one, does not have a good historical record for dealing with Eastern churches and in spite of Vatican II's guideline of "imposing no burden beyond what is indispensable" overtures from Rome are treated with some scepticism born out of negative historical experiences.

As we said above, the one factor which is simultaneously consoling and unsettling, is that ecumenists believe the movement is inspired and under the guidance of the Holy Spirit—which means anything can happen! One has only to think of the achievement of the World Council of Churches this century, or of how quickly the Roman Catholic Church moved from the dark days of *Mortalium Animos* to the surprise election of John XXIII, the *Decree on Ecumenism* and the current levels of cooperation with the World Council of Churches. Changes of heart like the examples just cited, are inspired from on-high and are the best reason for being optimistic about the future.

There are other issues which could be touched upon but this chapter has, I hope, highlighted some of the more serious issues and the work ahead on the way to a future united church, whatever form that might take.

* * *

Discussion Questions

1. Which issues do you think are important between churches, as you experience ecumenism?

2. Have you ever experienced proselytism? What are the principles at stake underlying this issue?

3. What is your idea of a new united church? What do you consider matters of church discipline rather than church doctrine?

4. What roles in ministry do women play in your church? Why do you think this is the case? Do you believe that the ordination of women is an obstacle to the churches reuniting?

Notes

1. Handout of the group at the General Assembly, Canberra, February 1991.
2. One exception to this would be the study of Mariology in Scripture, entitled *Mary in the New Testament: A Collaborative Assessment by Protestant and Roman Catholic Scholars*, London, Geoffrey Chapman, 1978, edited by R. Brown. The study was carried out by 4 Lutherans, 4 Roman Catholics, 2 Episcopalians, and 2 theologians from the Reformed tradition. The study was sponsored by the National Lutheran-Roman Catholic Dialogue in the USA.
3. Cf. also *Inter Insigniores*, SCDF, 1976, which stated the Roman Catholic case. For the exchange of letters on the ordination of women between Pope John Paul II, Archbishop Runcie and Cardinal Willebrands, cf. The Secretariat for Promoting Christian Unity, *Information Service*, 1986, No. 61 (III), pp. 106–111.
4. ARCIC I, *The Final Report*, London, CTS SPCK, 1982.
5. Lutheran–RC Committee, *Sacrament and Sacrifice*, Adelaide, Lutheran Publishing House, 1982.
6. Cf. *Baptism, Eucharist and Ministry*, Geneva, WCC, 1982, p. 11.
7. Ibid., Commentary (8), p. 11. This issue is pursued in great detail by B. Byron in his book, *Sacrifice and Symbol: A New Theology of The Eucharist for Catholic and Ecumenical Consideration*, Sydney, Catholic Institute of Sydney, 1991.
8. J. Honner, 'A New Ontology: Incarnation, Eucharist, Resurrection, and Physics', *Pacifica*, Vol. 4:1, Feb., 1991, pp. 15–50.
9. Cf. *Ecumenical Press Service*, 11–25 March 1991, 91.03.49.
10. Cf. *Declaration on the Position of the Catholic Church on the Celebration of the Eucharist in Common by Christians of Different Confessions*, SPUC, 1970; *Directory Concerning Ecumenical Matters*, Part One, SPUC, 1967, Part Two, SPUC, 1970; *On Admitting Other Christians to Eucharistic Communion in the Catholic Church*, SPUC, 1972; *Note Interpreting the*

"Instruction on Admitting Other Christians to Eucharistic Communion under Certain Circumstances", SPUC, 1973.

11. Also F. Sullivan, "Subsists in", *One in Christ*, Vol. XXII, No. 2, 1986, pp. 115–123.
12. Ibid. The chronicling of events is taken from this article, pp. 115–23.
13. Ibid., p. 116.
14. Cf. C. Willebrands, '"Subsists in": Vatican II's Ecclesiology of Communion', *One in Christ*, Vol. XXIII, No. 3, 1987, p. 183. The whole article traces the change in more depth, cf. pp. 179–91.
15. Cf. C. Hill, *The Mystery of Life*, Melbourne, Collins Dove, 1990, pp. 23–39.
16. Cf. P. Crow, 'Reflections on Models of Christian Unity', in *Living Today: Towards Visible Unity*, ed. T. Best, Geneva, WCC, 1988, pp. 21–38.
17. 22 February 1991.

CHAPTER SIX

Healing the Wounds: Current Dialogues

Our desire for mutual understanding and closer cooperation has for its foundation the basic conviction that in spite of many centuries of isolation from each other and the separate development of our two traditions, we nevertheless share an essentially common faith. (Coptic Pope Shenouda III and Anglican Archbishop Runcie, 1 October 1987)[1]

When I was in that land of saints and scholars—Ireland—not so long ago, I asked an elderly Roman Catholic parish priest of quite a large country town, how ecumenism was doing in his parish. He said something to the effect that ecumenism was being attended to, but mainly by the 'high-ups', by which I took it he meant the bishops and theologians. "Here", he added with a sigh, "we only have a handful of Protestants, and they are interested in nothing". I went away from the encounter slightly scandalized by his snap judgment on Protestants and wondering whether anyone had actually asked the handful of Protestants about their interests.

This story brings home to me how much more important it is to relate to people than it is to hold meetings and produce paper reports. The *Decree on Ecumenism* speaks about furthering the cause of ecumenism firstly by studying the history and customs of different churches, and secondly by entering into dialogue with them. We have touched upon the first part in the early chapters of this book. The second part is the challenge for everyone in a very practical way. In this chapter we will see what has been done by some international dialogues involving various churches and then attempt to answer the question: What can I do to promote ecumenism?

We know that entering into dialogue can be done by setting up committees of people competent to carry on such dialogues, the 'high-ups'. This competence might be taken to mean theological knowledge of one's own tradition at least. However this would be only one dimension. There are other important skills, such as the ability to relate easily to people, to listen, and to be flexible and open to other ideas. These skills were noticeably absent in people such as Humbert, Cerularius, Cajetan, Leo X and others. For ecumenism to prosper today there is a great demand for these skills.

Many people who have taken part in ecumenical dialogues have said that the most impressive and rewarding part of the dialogues has been the personal aspect—getting to know individuals and learning to pray together. This dimension is a qualitative aspect of dialogues which is not always immediately obvious. One tends to focus on the quantitative output of these dialogues, such as the number of "agreed statements" or reports that they produce. Dialogues are however not only about *paper*; more importantly, they are about *people* exploring a common faith, as Pope Shenouda and Archbishop Runcie point out in the quote above.

The lives of reports and statements start before, and go beyond, the publication date. It is a process. Acknowledging the valuable friendships that are made in the meetings and the theological insights gained is one thing. What is done with a report is what matters for the larger church membership. The best example is the *Baptism, Eucharist and Ministry* statement which has had an enormous impact on many churches in all parts of the world. Responses from churches have poured into Geneva and resulted in many volumes chronicling the replies of the various churches. However, even with this outstanding example, one must ask the question: Are the documents getting down to the ordinary Christian in the pew? My impression is that they are not.

In pursuing dialogues, there is a danger that churches do so at a level that excludes the ordinary Christian. Ways must be found to bridge the gap between the statements and the people. What is happening in the dialogues must, in some way, be brought to bear on the lives of ordinary church members.

The Challenges of Change.

Another danger is that dialogues could fragment the whole ecumenical movement. The description of the various dialogues gives the impression of multiple groups huddled into corners all over the world, earnestly discussing their commonalities and differences. I have no doubt that this is a necessary stage in the ecumenical movement, but only a stage. There has to be a coming together of churches in dialogue at some stage at the international level (such as happened at Lima), if endless repetition of topics is to be avoided. This also applies to bilateral dialogues at a state or national level. There is a need to broaden these dialogues out to the international level. This should not be difficult, and indeed is already happening, as many churches now have international representative bodies, such as the Baptist World Alliance or the Lutheran World Alliance.

Let us return for a moment to the point about stages in ecumenical dialogues. Not everyone, not every church, is at the same stage of ecumenical awareness and readiness. In addition, different groups will progress in their relationships at their own rate. It may be useful to see the dialogue as a developing relationship. This may help us to understand why some churches seem unwilling to join in even the most non-threatening ecumenical activity, while others are rushing ahead. A scale of interchurch relationships has even been evolved which is very helpful in this regard. It could be presented as follows:

conflict—competition—coexistence—cooperation—commitment—communion.

The progress along this continuum runs from left to right. The *conflict* stage is the one we have inherited from the time of the East–West Schism or Reformation. The stage of *communion* is hopefully our aim, as the Orthodox representatives have pointed out in Canberra, at the General Assembly in 1991. There is a danger in losing sight of the ultimate aim in working through the various stages. Let us now look at how some churches are working through these stages by way of dialogues.

International dialogues

As a brief indication of what is happening on the international level, we can look at some of the dialogues and the issues that are being discussed without attempting to be either comprehensive or exhaustive. One notes that the topics for discussion concern doctrine rather than morality. Issues of social morality such as nuclear war, disarmament, international trade and debt, or matters pertaining to more personal morality such as birth control, euthanasia, abortion, and homosexuality have not yet been widely addressed. They have however been the subject of discussions between the World Council of Churches and the Roman Catholic Church as we shall see below.[2]

By definition these dialogues are fluid and part of a process. It is never easy to report on a process as it is constantly evolving. What I propose to do here, is to take the rifts historically and ask the question, what is being done today to heal the wounds?

If we go back to problems resulting from the Council of Chalcedon, it is not surprising to find that the Orthodox families have been trying to do some reconciliation among themselves. As we saw, the family of Oriental Orthodox churches separated from the Christian (universal) Church at the Council of Chalcedon, and consequently from the Eastern Orthodox churches since the latter's beginnings in 1054. Since 1964, these two groups, the Eastern and Oriental Orthodox churches have been meeting informally. Initially they met in Aarhus, Denmark (1964), and then in Bristol (1967), Geneva (1970) and Addis Ababa (1971). In September 1990, an official joint commission of theologians and hierarchs, appointed by these two bodies, after an initial meeting at the monastery of Amba Bishoy in Egypt in 1989, signed an historic agreement at the Orthodox Center in Chambesy near Geneva. In this agreement they put an end to a centuries-old dispute on Christology which had divided these churches for 1500 years.[3]

To reinforce the seriousness of these dialogues, it is worth noting that at a meeting of the Eastern Orthodox patriarchs at the Phanar in Istanbul in March 1992, they alluded to a speedy reunion with the Oriental Orthodox churches.

The Christological debate that had divided them was centred on the issue of how one spoke about the natures of Christ. The Orientals (non-Chalcedonians at that time; Egypt, Syria and Palestine) spoke of "one incarnate nature" after the union of God and humanity in Christ. The Eastern Orthodox (Chalcedonians at that time; Constantinople, Rome) spoke instead of the incarnate Christ as being in two natures even after the union of divine and human natures.

There was mutual misunderstanding on this issue as we know from our history. Hence the Chalcedonians called the non-Chalcedonians, mono-physite (= one nature) while they in turn were called di-physites

(= two natures). Because of other non-theological reasons (one being that Rome and Constantinople resented the power of the Alexandrian patriarchate) they never really listened to what the opposition was trying to assert. They had poor interpersonal dialoguing skills, as we would say today. Each was trying to express the same mystery but in different ways.

Another contemporary dialogue that harkens back to Chalcedon is that between the Coptic and Roman Catholic churches. On 10 May 1973, Pope Paul VI of the Roman Catholic Church and Pope Shenouda III of the Coptic Orthodox Church while meeting in Rome for the first time in fifteen centuries, made a common declaration in which they, among other things, said they were setting up a joint Coptic Orthodox-Roman Catholic commission:

> To guide common study in the fields of Church tradition, patristics, liturgy, theology, history and practical problems, so that by cooperation in common we may seek to resolve, in a spirit of mutual respect, the differences existing between our Churches and be able to proclaim together the Gospel in ways which correspond to the authentic message of the Lord and to the needs and hopes of today's world.[4]

The restoration of friendship between these two churches, already underway since Vatican II, at which the Coptic Church had representatives, was made particularly emphatic by the handing back of the relics of St Mark in Venice to the Coptic Church on the occasion of the inauguration of St Mark's cathedral in Cairo, June 1968. As one can imagine, this gesture was an impressive symbol of reconciliation.

The first report of the joint commission (1974) contained a statement on Christology, which is not surprising given that the origins of the split date from the Christological doctrine of Chalcedon in 451, as we saw in Chapter Two. This was amplified in their 1976 report, which carried a Christological declaration. Subsequent meetings examined the role of councils in the life of the churches, sacraments, the See of Rome, and the need for further refinement of their guidelines. There was a break of ten years in meetings of the joint commission, which started afresh in 1988.

The 1988 meeting discussed the mystery of the Redemption, while the 1990 meeting focused, not surprisingly, on the sensitive *filioque* controversy from biblical, theological, patristic and historical perspectives. As we can see, there is an attempt to go back to those historical issues that caused the rift in the first place. In terms of the scale of ecumenical relationships, this dialogue has not lost sight of its ultimate aim. It continues with its 1979 aim in mind, i.e., "a full communion of faith expressing itself in communion in sacramental life and in the harmony of mutual relations between our two sister Churches in the one People of God".[5]

Also arising out of the ancient Christological debates, and worth mentioning in passing, is the embryonic dialogue between the Malankara Orthodox Syrian Church (of India) and the Roman Catholic Church (cf. Appendix C, for details of the Malankara Church). Their first meeting was in Kottayam (Kerala) in October 1989. As might well be expected, the topic of their first statement was the Incarnate Word, produced in June 1990.

The East–West rift: What is being done?

We said the first big rupture in Christianity was the East–West Schism of 1054. What is being done about that division in Christianity? As we saw at the end of Chapter Three, the meeting of Pope Paul VI and Patriarch Athenagoras I in 1964 provided the initial impetus for the subsequent Eastern Orthodox-Roman Catholic dialogue.

In 1980 the Joint International Commission for Theological Dialogue between the two churches was set up. This commission, in the words of Vatican II, has devoted itself "to the work of restoring the full communion that is desired between the Eastern Churches and the Catholic Church".[6] The first meeting of the commission was in Rhodes (on John's island of Patmos), and since then it has met virtually annually at Munich (twice), Nicosia, Crete, Opole (Poland), Bari (twice) and Valamo. It has produced two important statements, namely, *The Mystery of the Church and of the Eucharist in the light of the Mystery of the Holy Trinity*, and *Faith, Sacraments and the Unity of the Church*.[7] In 1988 it also produced a common statement with the rather unwieldy title of *The Sacrament of Order in the Sacramental Structure of the Church, with Particular Reference to the Importance of the Apostolic Succession for the Sanctification and Unity of the People of God*. This statement treats of the roles of bishop, priest and deacon in a traditional way and, as regards women, affirms that "our Churches remain faithful to the historical and theological tradition according to which they ordain only men to the priestly ministry" (#32).

Its current topic is "Ecclesiological and Canonical Consequences of the Sacramental Structure of the Church. Conciliarity and Authority in the Church".[8] This program has been upset in recent times with the political events of 1989 in Eastern Europe. With the freedom granted to religion to practise in public, the problem of what is called "uniatism" has arisen. Basically it concerns the Uniat churches that were forced to join the Russian Orthodox Church in 1946 under Stalin.

Prior to Stalin, and since the Council of Brest-Litovsk under King Sigismund III in 1596, they had enjoyed the freedom of being Eastern, yet Catholic in the sense that they accepted the pope. Yet this way of reading history is too simplistic. It would be closer to the truth to say that even in 1596, the bishops were more or less forced to vote in favor of joining up with Rome to avoid the persecution that the Protestants were undergoing. This uniatism lasted in some parts of Eastern Europe only until 1839, when Tsar Nicholas I dissolved it, either violently or non-violently, depending on what history one reads. What is sure is that the 'uniat problem' is like a festering sore in the Roman Catholic–Orthodox relationship and its origins go back much further than Stalin or even King Sigismund.

Thus 1989 saw the re-creation of these Uniat churches. The problem is that the Orthodox churches see this move in negative terms, as a sign that the Roman Catholic Church is not serious about the reunification of the churches. Uniatism, as perceived by the Orthodox, is the creation of churches affiliated to Rome whose *raison d'être* is to engage in proselytism among the Orthodox.[9] These feelings surfaced again at a meeting of Orthodox leaders, presided over by the Patriarch of Constantinople, Bartholomew I, in Istanbul in March 1992.[10]

Another negative incident was the withdrawal by the Patriarch of Jerusalem, in June 1989, of his church from all non-Orthodox dialogues because of alleged new doctrines and proselytism occurring under the umbrella of ecumenical goodwill. This latter seems to be a real problem in some areas. The Coptic-Roman Catholic and the Baptist-Roman Catholic dialogues have also seen fit to mention this in their recent common statements.

When attention is turned again to the topic of conciliarity and authority in the Church, some of the thorny issues awaiting this dialogue are issues like primacy, the papacy, the authority of synods, and the autonomy of sister churches.

The Reformation rift: What is being done?

The second big rift was the Protestant Reformation of the sixteenth century. We can now turn to the churches that sprung up at that time and see what initiatives have been taken at reconciliation involving these churches, the Roman Catholic Church and the Orthodox churches.

The Anglican-Lutheran International Continuation Committee has been meeting since the early 1970s. Recently they have been studying the question of the *episcope*, i.e., the role and function of the bishop in the Christian community. This is important because we know that not all Christian churches have bishops and many that do not are debating nowadays whether change is needed in this area. The result of Anglican-Lutheran discussions is found in the *Niagara Report* (1987), which, among other things, sees the bishop as providing in his office the link between the local and universal church.[11]

Other than with the Anglicans, the Lutherans have also been talking to the Roman Catholics. The Lutheran-Roman Catholic dialogue began in 1967 and has been directed at the goal of visible unity. It is sponsored by the Pontifical Council for Promoting Christian Unity and the Lutheran World Alliance, Geneva. They have produced six statements including *Ministry in the Church* (1982) and *Facing Unity* (1984), where they called for the churches to accept a reunification plan. Currently they are working on a statement on ecclesiology.

Another international initiative, well known by now, is the Anglican-Roman Catholic dialogue. It is referred to as the Anglican-Roman Catholic International Commission, or ARCIC for short. The first commission was called ARCIC I and it produced a number of agreed statements over the years. Here is a list of the year, title and place of each of the documents produced:

1971: Eucharistic Doctrine (Windsor)
1973: Ministry and Ordination (Canterbury)
1976: Authority in the Church I (Venice)
1981: Authority in the Church II (Windsor)

Each of these documents was discussed by the two sponsoring churches and as a result papers called "Elucidations" were published in 1979 and 1981. These, along with the other documents, are included in the book called *The Final Report*.[12]

It took the Roman Catholic Church ten years to reply officially to this ARCIC I report.[13] The reply praises many aspects of the report, especially the substantial agreement on the eucharist, but in other areas such as papal infallibility, the Marian dogmas and the Petrine ministry, it argues that there is no substantial agreement. One of the most worrying aspects of the reply is the underlying assumption that there is only one admissible way of saying things, the Roman way. Given that this is a bureaucratic reply, one cannot help asking if it has forgotten the Vatican II point about doctrine—that the deposit of faith is one thing, the way it is expressed another.

A second commission was constituted, ARCIC II, and it produced *Salvation and the Church* in 1987,[14] (which was an attempt to reach agreement on the doctrine of justification) and *Church as Communion* in 1990.[15] This latter document, as mentioned in Chapter One, explores the concept of the Church as *koinonia* in the Old and New Testaments, and the Church as a sacrament of salvation and sign of this *koinonia*. It also speaks of the Apostolicity, Catholicity and Holiness of the Church, in terms of the richness of diversity, the need to maintain a common apostolic faith, a shared sacramental life, a common ministry of oversight, and joint ways of reaching decisions and giving authoritative teaching. ARCIC II is continuing its task and currently preparing papers on ethics and the concept of reception.

A perhaps unlikely dialogue is that between the Baptist and Roman Catholic churches. Prior to Vatican II, these two churches were very far from being good friends. But in 1984 a 'conversation', sponsored by the Vatican Secretariat for Promoting Christian Unity and the Commission on Baptist Doctrine and Interchurch Cooperation of the Baptist World Alliance, was started in Berlin and then moved to Los Angeles, New York and, finally, Rome. Topics so far have included Evangelism, The Person and Work of Jesus Christ, Conversion and Discipleship, Proselytism, and Our Witness as Church. The 1988 report is entitled *Summons to Witness to Christ in Today's World*.[16]

Some dialogues have zeroed in on very practical issues. Such a dialogue has been the Methodist-Roman Catholic dialogue, initiated between the World Methodist Council and the Roman Catholic Church in 1967. It has met annually and reported every five years with a document. In 1971 the *Denver Report* dealt with a very broad sweep of topics such as Christianity and the contemporary world, spirituality, Christian home and family, eucharist, ministry and authority. Some of these topics were revisited in the *Dublin Report* of 1975 which went

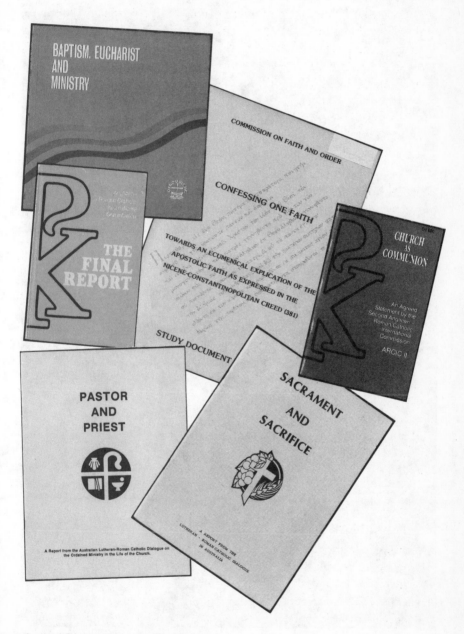

Some Contemporary Documents.

Ecumenism is about people.

in greater depth into spirituality, world issues, the doctrine of the eucharist and the ordained ministry. The Holy Spirit was the subject of the 1981 *Honolulu Report.*

In 1985 the *Nairobi Report* tackled the question of the nature of the Church. This report noted the similarities in the order and structure of the two churches, but also the differences such as in the ministry of the teaching office.[17]

We know from history that the Reformed churches and the Roman Catholics have never got on very well, yet the Reformed-Roman Catholic International Dialogue has been meeting since 1970 in the prevailing ecumenical spirit. The meetings are sponsored by the World Alliance of the Reformed Churches and the Pontifical Commission for Promoting Christian Unity. Their statements have been: "The Presence of Christ in the Church and World"; "The Theology of Marriage and the Problem of Mixed Marriages"; and "Towards a Common Understanding of the Church".

With a much lower profile, the Disciples of Christ-Roman Catholic dialogue has been meeting annually since 1977. In 1989 its theme was "The Involvement of the Whole Church in Handing on the Apostolic Tradition".[18]

In the category of unexpected get-togethers, top billing would have to go to the Pentecostal-Roman Catholic International Dialogue. The fact that these two churches came together for ecumenical conversations is striking by any standards. One side (Catholic) consisted of official representatives of their church, whereas the Pentecostal team came together by personal invitation of David du Plessis. There was much opposition to any contact with Catholics on the part of some Pentecostals. On occasions du Plessis could not remember whom he had invited and who had accepted. One church is the biggest Christian church, the other the fastest growing revivalist movement. Hosken refers to their meetings as "this unusual creature of the ecumenical world".[19]

They started dialoguing in 1972. The aims of the dialogue were expressed in various ways. "A dialogue on spirituality", "to share principles of the life of prayer and principles of life in the Spirit", and "to increase mutual understanding", were some of the expressions used. In 1986 they met in Pasadena, California. Referring not only to this meeting, but to the whole dialogue to date, Hosken maintains the dialogue has resulted in "encouraging, cajoling, and even needling the Pentecostal denominations into a reconsideration of their historic rejection and hatred for everything Catholic".[20] On the Catholic side, they have learnt a lot about the Pentecostal movement and the importance of giving emphasis to narrative theology, spiritual experience, giving testimony and the exercise of spiritual gifts.

Their fourth meeting was in Emmetten, Switzerland in 1988 and 1989. The theme was *koinonia* and baptism. The meeting in 1990 (also in Emmetten), which marked the first session of the fourth phase of their meetings, took up the theme of evangelization.

Although we have been considering bilateral dialogues in the form of individual churches, one should not forget the World Council of Churches-Roman Catholic cooperation. Following Vatican II the two bodies set up the Joint Working Group in 1965. In 1990, celebrating twenty-five years of cooperation, this group published its sixth report, which gives a useful summary of its activities since the Vancouver Assembly of 1983. Not only does it give an overview of the past but it looks to the future as well.

What kind of activities has this joint group been engaged in? Its activities related to four areas:

1. *Unity of the Church—the Goal and the Way.* This produced two written documents, entitled "The Church: Local and Universal" and "The Hierarchy of Truths". Both documents are very useful in any ecumenical dialogue because of the importance of the issues they raise. These two statements are very theological; of a more practical nature are some of the other topics it has discussed, for example, the potential sources of division, especially ethical issues such as abortion, contraception, homosexuality and euthanasia; the impact of Council of Churches on the ecumenical movement; and the pastorally sensitive issue of Christian mixed marriages.

2. *Ecumenical Formation.* Significantly the report only has two paragraphs on this. This is a neglected area in the ecumenical movement, at least from a local perspective. A study document is in the pipeline and hopefully this area will receive greater priority in the future. The report says it would like this to be the case.

3. *Common Witness.* Here its major thrust has been in the promotion of the Week of Prayer for Christian Unity and in collaboration on the topic of Justice, Peace and the Integrity of Creation.

4. *Social Thought and Action.* Its work has been on basic issues such as development and the debt crisis, racism and apartheid, armaments and arms transfers, human rights and religious liberty.

Looking to the future, the Joint Working Group would like to see its agenda more limited in scope and sees as priorities: the ecclesiological dimensions of ecumenical work: ecumenical education and formation; and, common witness and mission. The criticism levelled at the Joint Working Group is that it tends to *talk* about issues but takes very little action. There is a built-in problem here with the Vatican often preferring, for political and diplomatic reasons, to talk in generalities on social issues, whereas the World Council of Churches tends to be very prophetic and specify the details. The nature and structure of the two bodies are also so different that giving combined social witness has been a persistent problem.

Now we come to dialogues sponsored by the World Council of Churches. A number of documents has been produced by the various bodies. As we mentioned above, one of the most popular, produced by the Faith and Order Commission of the World Council of Churches in Geneva (of which the Roman Catholic Church is a full member, but not of the WCC itself), is the document entitled *Baptism, Eucharist and Ministry* (1982).[21] It is also known as the 'Lima text' because the work was finally approved at a meeting in Lima, Peru. It was an impressive achievement because the spectrum of Christian churches involved in the writing of the text was so great. It has become a very popular document for study and as the title suggests, it addresses fundamental Christian issues such as baptism, eucharist and ministry. The way the document is written and published is interesting. It has columns of text and, where appropriate, a parallel "commentary" column for an explanation of a particular matter, to point out some differences between the churches, or to suggest further study of those issues.

A follow-up document to this, which is currently at the stage of a "Study Document" is entitled *Confessing One Faith* (1987).[22] Here the focus has moved to the basic Christian creed, as the subtitle indicates: "Towards an Ecumenical explication of the Apostolic Faith as expressed in the Nicene-Constantinopolitan creed (381)". Christians are invited to read the document and to send their responses to the Faith and Order Commission in Geneva. Each phrase or part of the creed is dealt with in the same way—firstly the text of the creed, then its biblical foundation, and lastly an explication of the text for today. The purpose of the document is, as the introduction says:

> to stimulate further and broaden this cooperation [between churches] so that the document can be improved during the

coming years with the help of insights, comments and suggestions from a wider process of reflection in the ecumenical community.[23]

What we have seen in the dialogues referred to shows an enormous amount of goodwill and energy on the part of so many churches in seeking to redress the disunity which all Christians have inherited historically. Much has been achieved already by way of breaking the ice and making friendships, but also in terms of beginning to listen to and understand other points of view in matters of church discipline as well as doctrine. As in the case of the Christological misunderstandings of the fifth century, some have been able to be cleared up relatively quickly. Others pose bigger problems.

The task ahead is enormous but the momentum has been established. It is only to be expected that the movement towards unity will, like any process, have its moments of quick visible advance as well as its plateaux of consolidation. Success is ultimately assured though if the priority of people over paper is maintained. It is a sobering thought that Humbert in 1054 did not bother to meet with Cerularius. He was overkeen on placing the piece of paper that was the bull of excommunication on the altar of Sancta Sophia.

Fine and necessary as these international dialogues are, it must be a concern to all that often the average parishioner (and minister or priest) does not hear about them. To my mind there is still a huge gap between the people involved in the dialogues and their reports on the one hand, and the parishioners in the pews on the other hand. Let us be honest. For most parishioners the dialogues and reports might just as well have been conducted on a different planet for all they know. Some strategies for bringing the two together have got to be thought out. Presently few seem particularly interested in this problem.

* * *

Discussion questions

1. Are you involved with any church group in local dialogues or prayer meetings? If so, where would you see yourself in terms of the scale of relationships as shown on page 122?

2. Are you aware of any of the dialogues going on between churches? If you are, what impact have they had on you or your local church? If you have not been aware of these dialogues, why do you suppose that is?

3. Do you think the ecumenical movement has slowed down in recent years? What evidence do you have for your opinion?

Notes

1. Cf. *One in Christ*, Vol. XXIII, No. 4, 1987, p. 341.
2. Cf. T. Derr, *Barriers to Ecumenism: The Holy See and the World Council on Social Questions*, New York, Orbis Books, 1983.
3. Cf. K. M. George, "Historic reconciliation", *One World*, No. 167, July 1991, pp. 4–6.
4. The whole issue of *Information Service*, No. 76, 1991 (I), is devoted to the documents of the Roman Catholic Church and the Coptic Orthodox Church (1973–1988). This quote is found on p. 9.
5. Ibid., p. 33.
6. W. Abbott, (ed.), *Documents of Vatican II*, London, Geoffrey Chapman, 1966, "Decree on Ecumenism", #14.
7. Cf. "Faith, Sacrament and the Unity of the Church", *One in Christ*, 1987: 4, pp. 330–40.
8. *Information Service*, No. 68, 1988 (III–IV), pp. 160–1.
9. Cf. C. Davey, "Clearing a path through a minefield: Orthodox-RC dialogue (2)", *One in Christ*, Vol. XXVII, No. 1, 1991, pp. 8-33.
10. *The Tablet*, 21 March 1992, p. 384.
11. Cf. G. Evans, "Niagara Report on Episcope and Episcopacy", *One in Christ*, Vol. XXV, No. 3, 1989, pp. 281–6.
12. ARCIC I, *The Final Report*, London, CTS/SPCK, 1982.
13. Cf. 'The Vatican Response to ARCIC I', *The Tablet*, 7 December 1991, pp. 1521–4.
14. ARCIC II, *Salvation and the Church*, Sydney, AIO Press, 1987.
15. Cf. *One in Christ*, Vol. XXVII, No. 1, 1991; also E. Yarnold, "The Church as Communion", *The Tablet*, 26 January 1991, p. 118.
16. *Information Service*, No. 72, 1990, pp. 5–13; text also provided in *One in Christ*, Vol. XXII, No. 3, 1990, pp. 238–55.
17. Cf. *Information Service*, No. 62, 1986 (IV), pp. 206–15; also see "Towards a Statement on the Church", *One in Christ*, Vol. XXII, No. 3, 1986, pp. 241–66.
18. "Ecumenical News", *Information Service*, No. 69, 1989 (1), p. 20.
19. P. Hosken, "Dialogue Extraordinary", *One In Christ*, Vol. XVIV, No. 3, 1988, pp. 202–13.
20. Ibid., p. 212. The value of this dialogue is brought home in Jerry L. Sandidge's book, *Roman Catholic/Pentecostal Dialogue (1977-1982): A Study in Developing Ecumenism*, 2 Vols, Frankfurt am Main, Verlag Peter Lang, 1987. Sandidge is a minister of the American Assemblies of God.

21. *Baptism, Eucharist, and Ministry*, Faith and Order Paper No. 111, Geneva, WCC, 1982. The official Roman Catholic response to this document is entitled, *Baptism, Eucharist and Ministry: An Appraisal*, cf. *Origins*, 1987, pp. 401–416.
22. *Confessing One Faith*, Faith and Order Paper No. 140, Geneva, WCC, 1987.
23. Ibid., p. 1.

CHAPTER SEVEN

YOU AND I: SOME PRACTICAL HINTS

Having spoken about ecumenism by the 'high-ups', in the words of the Irish parish priest, it is time to turn to what the ordinary person is doing and can do to promote ecumenism. Ecumenism at the international or macro level is ultimately going to come to nothing unless the church members make it work. My impressions at the moment are that, although small groups of people are working hard at establishing a new ecumenical spirit in their parishes, by and large the congregations are yet to be won over to this new ecumenical enthusiasm. Some conservative Roman Catholics and others would see it as some newfangled idea that came in with Vatican II.

What can be done by ordinary persons, given that international conferences are never going to be their way of contributing? I want to keep to suggestions that are, more or less, within the capacity of the ordinary individual. Hence I will omit suggestions about organizing adult education speakers on ecumenical topics, or the exchange of pulpits, as these are normally outside the ordinary parishioner's capacity to organize. Here are some simple possibilities.

Prayer or Spiritual Ecumenism

This is an obvious one but bears repetition. Other than private prayer for unity, one obvious path to follow is the one to make something special out of the annual Week of Prayer for Christian Unity in one's home or parish, or both.

Where prayers are composed each Sunday for the service, mention can be made regularly of ecumenical events and aspects to pray for.

Attending Sunday Worship

This is something practical that anyone can do by themselves. The idea is to attend a Sunday worship in a church *other than one's own denomination*, and get to know how they worship, preach and generally get a feel for the way they practise their Christianity. This strategy is a guaranteed way of awakening awareness of other traditions.

Bible Study and Discussion Groups

These can be organized at the local level and involve two or more churches. The idea is to study and pray together in order to get to know each other better. The group can decide what it will choose for study. It might be some scripture readings, the readings for the Sunday, for example, or some study material creatively put together by ecumenical councils. Not only is the material studied, but also discussed and then prayed about. The discussion part is meant to be a sharing of insights and understandings which will mean hearing opinions with which one might feel inclined to disagree. But the point of the discussions is not to prove one's point correct and others wrong. Differences of opinions should be understood and noted but not argued out at these meetings.

The praying together is important if the group is to get to know each other and listen to the inspiration of the Holy Spirit. The prayer section should never be left out. These evenings, or days, could last from one to two hours, and might end socially with some refreshment.

These groups work best with about ten to fifteen persons. If the numbers are bigger it might be advisable to have two groups. Can these groups be organized by the individual? If nothing is happening in a parish, any individual could contact a few friends and then approach another Christian church and seek anyone who would be interested in having a Bible study together. Ministers should be kept informed of the group's activities but their attendance is not essential for the success of the group.

Sharing Services or Worship

From time to time combined services can be organized. What is organized and the format it takes will depend on the churches taking part. One of the easiest is the traditional annual Christmas carols service. There would be very few Christian churches, I would hope, that could not join in a combined singing of carols and readings from Scripture. However the pride of place should go to the most important feast of the Christian calendar, namely, Easter. Combined dawn Easter services are becoming very popular in some countries. It is a marvellous way for Christians to affirm their mutual faith.

Another form of combined worship might take the form of scripture readings, hymns, prayers and a sermon from an invited preacher on a theme relevant to ecumenism.

The question is, who organizes these services? Admittedly individuals cannot organize these by themselves. One needs an interchurch group or some small committee of like-minded individuals to get the cooperation of two to three ministers.

An example of what can be done is the German *Kirchentag*. It is held every two years or so and originally started as an independent lay movement. Mainly attended by thousands of young people, it is a church festival with dancing and music, aimed at bringing Christians together to strengthen their faith and encourage them to witness in the world. It also helps to create awareness of belonging to a worldwide fellowship of Christians.

Combined Social Action

This could be on any social justice issue relevant to the local churches and might take the form of a prayer meeting, demonstration march, collecting signatures, holding a protest meeting or whatever. It may mean hiring a bus to go and participate in a peace march, demonstrating against the government organizing a trade fair in arms, or visiting poor areas deprived of running water and other facilities.

Today there are nearly 20 million refugees in the world. Some people from different denominations have come together to help refugees settle into their new country. Many skills are required, from looking for accommodation to finding furniture and cooking utensils. Many hands are required. This seems a very practical and beautiful way for Christians to demonstrate their adherence to gospel values in today's world.

Again individuals can organize themselves by simply picking up the phone or calling on people. What is required in all these things are people who are self-starters. Ministers of religion are busy people and waiting for them to take all the initiatives can never work.

Participation in Simply Sharing Week

Where this is part of the ecumenical calendar, the idea is to live simply for a week so that others can simply live. The money that is saved through, for example, eating less at some meals, is sent to a worthwhile relief or development agency. Through this practice some degree of empathy and sensitivity is developed for our brothers and sisters throughout the world.

Interchurch Fundraising Functions

This is simple enough. Let me give an example of the most basic approach. We had a small interchurch discussion group going and found we wanted to raise some money for the poor of the district, especially during the tough times of the recession when many people were put out of work.

All that was needed was for members of the group to promise cakes, contact others for cakes, and get permission from the local council to set up a store on a Saturday morning at the local shopping area. Now comes the interesting bit. A banner was drawn up saying who the group was. Local people for the first time noticed that the churches were doing something together, and this will hopefully get people thinking and joining in. In carrying out this simple project, members of the different churches had to work and organize together. All this helps people to get to know each other better.

Becoming a Financial Contributor to Ecumenical Relief Agencies

There are now agencies for the collection and distribution of funds that are interchurch by nature. Being a contributor to one of these can promote ecumenism by keeping the cooperative enterprise going and also by helping oneself and others to think ecumenically. Often newsletters or brochures from these agencies supply information about how the money is being spent which is concrete information on how the churches are collaborating.

Subscribing to an Ecumenical Magazine

This would be of interest to the person who wants to know more about interchurch happenings, but will also be a valuable way of introducing ecumenism to neighbours and friends who might know nothing about it. On the international level there are three worth mentioning, *Ecumenical Press Service*, *One World*, and *Information Service*.[1] National and local bodies would also have their own publications, such as *The Tablet*, *The Month* and *One in Christ* (U.K.), *National Outlook* (Australia), *Ecumenism* (Canada), *Ecumenist* and *Ecumenical Courier* (U.S.A.).

Local Ecumenical Projects

Another initiative, not within the capacity of the individual to bring about but worth reporting, is the phenomenon known as a Local Ecumenical Project, or LEP for short. LEPs are well known in the United Kingdom in particular, Milton Keynes in England being one such example. A LEP happens when at least two Christian congregations decide to work closely together and formalize their agreement by writing it down. They occur for a variety of reasons. In some cases they arise from being in new areas with unique opportunities for collaboration; or from pragmatic reasons such as declining numbers and resources. Sometimes they simply arise out of people's conviction that they are called to work together in pursuing God's mission.

The kind of sharing that occurs in a LEP can vary greatly, from sharing a building to sharing a common pastor. One example of sharing pastors comes from Scotland. In 1986, five denominations, the Methodists, United Reformed, and Reformed (Church of Scotland, Congregational Union, United Free) signed an agreement that "ministers of all churches may exercise all aspects of their ministries, including the celebration of the sacraments, in any of these churches when invited to do so and in accordance with the recognized procedures of these churches".[2] On other occasions congregations might have common chaplaincies (prison, hospital or university), youth clubs, or marriage preparation classes. The important thing to grasp is that there are many forms of local ecumenical cooperation.

When churches write down their agreements to cooperate they are said "to covenant". One of the important implications of these covenants is that ecumenism moves away from being seen as an extra option to one's religious life, to becoming integral to being Christian.

* * *

Notes

1. *Ecumenical Press Service* and *One World* are published by the WCC, Box 2100, CH-1211, Geneva 2, Switzerland; and *Information Service* by the Pontifical Council for Promoting Christian Unity, Vatican City, via dell'Erba, 21-00193, Rome, Italy.
2. *Ecumenical Press Service*, 86.02.42.

Activities for Further Ecumenical Learning

These activities can be used with a group or class, as is appropriate, and modified as circumstances demand.

Discussions

Here are some possible topics for debate or discussion. Some topics lend themselves to assigning two groups different denominational affiliation, for example, imagine one half are Orthodox arguing against the ordination of women, the other half Anglicans arguing for it; or Baptists in favour of believer's baptism and Catholics against it, etc. The idea is to gain added insight into different viewpoints—not to become acrimonious!

- Should women be ordained?
- Infant baptism versus believer's baptism.
- Communion under both species?
- Luther versus Cajetan on indulgences.
- Should a united church have a pope-figure?
- The big divisions in today's world are not those between religious denominations, but between the RICH and the POOR nations.
- Add your own topics to this list.

Creative thinking!

Imagine your ideal united Christian church of the future.
- What elements of the faith and of morals would all members have to agree on?
- What elements would be flexible and allow for cultures and customs?
- What organizational and ministerial structures would it have?

Interview

Conduct an interview with your local minister or priest, parishioner or anyone else. Ask:
- What does ecumenism mean for you?
- Why bother about ecumenism?
- What is the future of ecumenism?

Report back to your group.

Visit

Visit another Christian church for a service. Note all details about the service: readings, prayers, singing, order of service, sermon, communion, participation of congregation, seating, icons or statues, holy pictures, arrangement of the furniture in the church.

Report back to your group about your visit.

Music

- Select pieces of music that illustrate aspects of ecumenism for you. Play the music for your group and describe why it appeals to you.
- Take the hymn "One Bread, One Body" and explain the words in the context of ecumenism.

● Choose a modern song whose words speak to you about aspects of ecumenism.

Art

Do a painting or drawing which symbolizes ecumenism, or some aspects of ecumenism, for you. Describe the symbolism for others in the group.

Literature

The English poet John Milton (1608–1674) was secretary to Oliver Cromwell. He wrote a poem to commemorate a persecution of the (Protestant) Waldensians which took place in Piedmont, northern Italy, in the seventeenth century. It was Cromwell's threat of military intervention that ended the persecution. In his role as secretary, Milton drafted letters of protest which Cromwell sent to the Protestant countries of Europe. The text of this commemorative poem is as follows:

Sonnett XVIII
On the late Massacre in Piedmont[1]
Avenge, O Lord, thy slaughtered saints, whose bones
Lie scattered on the Alpine mountains cold,
Ev'n them who kept thy truth so pure of old
When all our fathers worshipped stocks and stones,
Forget not; in thy book record their groans
Who were thy sheep, and in their ancient fold
Slain by the bloody Piemontese that rolled
Mother with infant down the rocks. Their moans
The Vales redoubled to the hills, and they
To heav'n. Their martyred blood and ashes sow
O'er all th'Italian fields, where still doth sway
The triple tyrant, that from these may grow
A hundredfold, who, having learnt thy way,
Early may fly the Babylonian woe.

* * *

- Who is said to have the truth in this poem? Who among Christians has the truth today?
- How are the Piedmontese described?
- How did Christians justify persecution in those days?
- What happens to the "moans" of the slain?
- What happens to the blood and ashes of those martyred according to the poet?
- Who is the "triple tyrant"? Do you think this criticism was valid in those days? What about today?
- What is the "Babylonian woe" mentioned in the last line?
- Give your reasons for liking or not liking this poem.

Creative writing

Write your own poem about any aspects of unity or ecumenism you wish. As a help, think of those aspects about which you feel strongly. Share your poem with the group.

Note
1.   Milton, *Poetical Works*, ed. D. Bush, Oxford, OUP, 1966, p. 198.

Thumbnail Sketches of the Protestant Reformers

Bucer, Martin (1491–1551)

He was a German Protestant moderate reformer, born in Schlettstadt in Alsace. He joined the Dominicans in 1506 and ten years later met Luther and Erasmus in Heidelberg. He apostatized in 1521, married and settled in Strasbourg. Henry VIII consulted him about his divorce from Catherine of Aragon. Later in 1549, Cranmer invited him to become the Regius Professor of Divinity at Cambridge. He had some influence on the English Prayer Book of 1552. Known as the reformer of Strasbourg, he spent much time trying to reconcile the Zwinglians and the Lutherans. Luther called him a "chatterbox". He taught that in the eucharist Christ was given not *in* or *under* the forms of bread and wine, but *with* them, known as *receptionism*. Calvin worked under him in Strasbourg when he was exiled from Geneva in the period, 1538–1541. He helped to introduce the system of discipline by pastors and elders that Calvin later applied so well in Geneva.

Bullinger, Heinrich (Henry) (1504–1575)

This Swiss reformer succeeded Zwingli at Zurich after the battle at Cappell in 1531. He was born at Bremgarten and went to a school run by the Brethren of the Common Life at Emmerich. This was followed by humanistic training at the university of Cologne. He studied Luther's works at Cologne and also studied under Zwingli for a time. In 1529, the year he married Anna Adlischwiler, he was made pastor of Bremgarten, which he converted to Protestantism. When Zwingli was killed at Cappell he took refuge in Zurich and became chief pastor there. He was a prodigious writer.

Calvin, Jean (John) (1509–1564)

He was born in Noyon in France and lost his mother when he was six years old. He studied Latin and theology at the university of Paris and law at Orleans. Somewhere between 1532 and 1534 he underwent a sudden conversion and embraced the doctrine of the Protestant reformers. He retreated to Basel and wrote, in 1536, *The Institute of the Christian Religion*, Protestantism's greatest theological work. On his travels he was passing through Geneva when Farel persuaded him to stay. He was employed there as a teacher and preacher. From 1538 to 1541 he was exiled from Geneva because of his rigid methods of reform. He was recalled in 1541 and remained there until his death in 1564. He married the widow of an Anabaptist, Idelette de Bure, in 1540.

Farel, Guillaume (William) (1489–1565)

He was a Frenchman of similar background to Calvin. He was born near Gap in Dauphiné, France. He was converted to Protestantism while studying in Paris. In 1523 he went to Basel to avoid arrest. During the period 1533–8 he was a preacher in Geneva while his friend Calvin was the organiser. Both were expelled from Geneva. Calvin later returned but Farel went to Neuchatel and remained there as pastor to the end of his life.

Knox, John (1513–1572)

He was a Scottish reformer, inspiring preacher and prophet. He was born at Morham or Giffordgate, Haddington. When Mary Tudor became Queen in 1553, Knox fled to the Continent and to Geneva where he spent most of the next 18 months. He returned to Scotland in 1555 and denounced the many abuses of the Church in Scotland with great courage and determination. He married Mary Bowes in 1556. The same year he returned to Geneva, this time for three years. He referred to Geneva under Calvin as "the most perfect school of Christ that ever was on earth since the days of the Apostles". In 1559 he finally returned to Scotland and through his zeal helped to establish Calvinism, known as Presbyterianism in Scotland. His first wife died in 1560. Four years later he married Margaret Stewart. He died in Edinburgh in 1572.

Luther, Martin (1483–1546)

He is the first and most important figure among the reformers. He was born in Eisleben, Saxony, of peasant parents. His father was a copper miner. He studied at Erfurt University and, after an experience in a thunderstorm, he joined the Augustinians and became a very conscientious, if scrupulous monk. Obtaining his doctorate in 1512, he lectured in Scripture at the university of Wittenberg. It was here that he denounced the corruption in the Church, especially the sale of indulgences. He preached justification by faith alone. He publicized his ninety-five theses in Wittenberg in 1517 and after a long and futile period of attempted reconciliation, he was excommunicated in 1520. He married Catherine van Bora in 1524. The Augsburg Confession of 1530 is the basis of the Lutheran confession of Christianity.

Melanchthon, Philipp (1497–1560)

His original name was Schwarzerd (black earth) but took the Greek name Melanchthon, as many did in the age of the Renaissance. He was Luther's assistant. He was born at Bretten, Baden, and educated at Heidelberg, and in 1512 went to Tübingen. Later he became professor of Greek at Wittenberg where he met Luther. In 1530 he made a valuable contribution to Protestantism in the Augsburg Confession. He was a peacemaker, trying, among other things, to reconcile Bucer and Calvin over eucharistic doctrine.

Oecolampadius, Johannes (1482–1531)

His original name was Husschyn, Hussgen, or Henssgen. He was born in Weinsberg in the Palatinate in 1482. He was educated at Bologne, Heidelberg, Stuttgart and Tübingen. He knew Latin, Greek and Hebrew. In 1523 he was appointed professor at the university of Basel and promoted the cause of the Reformation. He defended the eucharistic doctrine of his friend Zwingli. After 1529 he supervised the reform of the Basel church until his death.

Zwingli, Huldreich, Huldrych, or Ulrich (1484–1531)

He was a Swiss reformer from Zurich. He was born at Wildhaus, St Gallen, and of peasant extraction. He studied at Bern, Vienna and Basel, and was found to be a gifted musician and singer. He joined the Dominicans in 1497 but was soon withdrawn by his parents and in 1506 became parish priest of Glarus. In 1516 he became preacher to the Benedictine monastery at Einsiedeln where he denounced the pilgrimages to the shrine of the Blessed Virgin. Back in Zurich at the Grössmunster in 1519, he began attacking Catholic doctrine, declaring Scripture the sole rule of faith. He removed sacred images and pictures from churches. He declared the eucharist merely symbolic. In 1522 Zwingli married Anna Reinhard. He was killed at Cappell in combat against the Catholic Forest Cantons. His position was more extreme than Luther or the English reformers. The success of Calvinism largely limited his influence to Switzerland. A meeting with Luther at Marburg in 1529 to resolve their dispute over the Real Presence was unsuccessful.

APPENDIX C

The Oriental Orthodox Churches

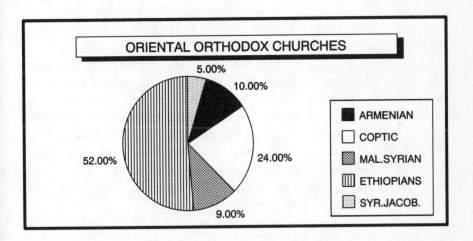

ORIENTAL ORTHODOX CHURCHES

- 5.00%
- 10.00%
- 24.00%
- 9.00%
- 52.00%

ARMENIAN
COPTIC
MAL.SYRIAN
ETHIOPIANS
SYR.JACOB.

The Armenian Apostolic Church

Historical background

Tradition says that the Apostles (Thaddeus and Bartholomew) brought Christianity to ancient Armenia, which is why this church is called the "Armenian Apostolic Church". Subsequently, through the efforts of

153

Gregory the Illuminator in 301, it was espoused as the religion of the state, making Armenia the oldest Christian kingdom. Its liturgies and customs are therefore very ancient and respected.

At the time of the Russian Revolution (1917), the use of "apostolic", not "orthodox", in the title of this church proved useful as it prevented the Russian authorities from forcing it to join the Russian Orthodox Church as they did with other churches such as the Ukrainian Orthodox. Presentday Armenia is only one-tenth its original size. It is bounded by Georgia to the north, which is Christian, but Azerbaijan, Iran, and Turkey are all Muslim countries. The original Armenia comprised the present Armenian (previously 'Soviet Socialist') Republic, adjacent parts of the previous 'Soviet' Azerbaijan (Nagorno-Karabakh, Nakhichevan), the north-eastern provinces of Turkey, and the western parts of Irian Azerbaijan.

After the Treaty of Berlin in 1878, the Armenians agitated for their own independence, as the great powers had done nothing to promote their aspirations. The great bone of contention in the years that followed was the attempted genocide committed on the Armenian people by the Turks between 1894 and 1922, which resulted in about 1.5 million people being put to death and the same number resettled. The Turks have denied that it took place. The Armenians want them to acknowledge that it occurred and apologize. The alleged reason for resettling the Armenians was that they were near the border with Russia at the time of the First World War and siding with them. During the First World War many Armenians fled into various countries including Syria, Jordan, Lebanon, Egypt, Iraq, Iran, Europe and the USA. Today Los Angeles has a huge Armenian population.

There is also an Armenian Church, called the Catholic Armenian Church, that is united with Rome.

Church life

Armenians accept only the first three Ecumenical Councils—Nicea (325), Constantinople (381) and Ephesus (431)—but not Chalcedon (451). They are said by some to be monophysite because they tend to fuse the human and divine natures into one. However they do not see themselves as monophysite.

Their clergy may marry before ordination but only celibates become part of the hierarchy. This practice is being reviewed. The Catholicos is elected by a group of one-third clergy and two-thirds laity. The

Supreme Patriarch and Catholicos of All Armenians has oversight of the Armenian catholicosate of Cilicia (nowadays in Lebanon), and the patriarchates of Constantinople and Jerusalem. Another of his duties is to bless the Holy Oil for use in all churches and to ordain bishops.

The common language of church members is Armenian, an Indo-European language with thirty-six characters, which the children learn at Saturday school. There is also the classical language which is used in the liturgies.

Armenians have seven sacraments—baptism, confirmation, communion, confession, holy matrimony, priesthood, extreme unction.

***

Coptic Orthodox Church

Historical background

A member of the Oriental or "non-Chalcedonian" group of churches, they take their origin from St Mark, who was the first bishop of Alexandria in Egypt (68). Pope Shenouda III, the 117th successor to St Mark, is their patriarch, and resides in the ancient see of Alexandria. He with sixty-three bishops forms the Holy Synod of the Coptic Church. They are incorrectly said to be Eutycheans or monophysite, since they have always believed in God Incarnate with his divinity and humanity fully present and united without mixture, confusion or change.

The Abyssinian Coptic Church (or Abyssinian Ethiopian Church) used to be under the authority of the Coptic Church of Egypt, but is now independent. Its patriarch is Basilius, who resides in Addis Ababa.

The Coptic Church uses Arabic in Egypt, and occasionally Coptic. The word "Coptic" comes from the religious name of the old capital Memphis "Hakuptak" which led to the Greek word "Aigyptos", meaning Egyptian. Since all the Christian Egyptians were under the Roman Empire, the word "Copt" was used in reference to Egyptians in general, and later for the Egyptian Christians only (currently about 8 million in Egypt).

The patriarch is Pope Shenouda III. They are also found in USA, Canada, UK, Germany, France, Austria, Australia, and of course in Egypt, Sudan, Ethiopia (branch of Coptic Orthodox) and Kenya.

Church life

There are seven sacraments. As regards baptism, infant baptism is practised by threefold immersion, after which the eucharist and Holy Chrism are received. Reconciliation/confession is another sacrament, with counselling for those who need it. Daily reception of the eucharist is encouraged. There is anointing when someone is sick. The other sacraments are marriage and priesthood.

As is the case with other Oriental churches, priests may marry before ordination. Their work is pastoral and focussed on the parish. Deacons may also be married. Bishops however are taken from the ranks of the monks and are not married.

The liturgy is celebrated in Arabic (Egyptian Arabic, which is not the same as Lebanese Arabic), with some Coptic and English where appropriate. The Coptic language used to be the only liturgical language until the seventh century when the Muslims imposed Arabic. Easter is celebrated on the Sunday immediately following the Jewish Passover.

The Sunday liturgy takes about four hours, and the liturgy of St Basil is followed. The men sit on one side of the church and women on the other. Much incense is used in the Mass and singing is continuous. It is a very ancient church—for centuries it was cut off from the rest of Christendom and has therefore preserved original liturgies and customs almost intact.

The favourite saints are St Mark, St George, John the Baptist, St Bishoy (monk), Mary, the Archangel Michael, St Anthony. St Bishoy was an Egyptian desert monk who lived in the 4th century. In the West he was known as St Christopher (who was dropped from the Roman calendar in 1969). The Copts often have pictures in their house of the Last Supper or Crucifixion, or of Apostles. They use prayer beads and repeat the prayer, "Lord have mercy".

Fasting is practised from midnight before the feast, and before every time communion is received. Other periods of fasting are: 55 days for Lent; 40 days before Christmas; after Pentecost and before the feast of St Peter and Paul; 15 days before the Feast of the Assumption on 22 August. Every Wednesday and Friday are fast days as well, except during the holy fifty days that follow Easter, including Christmas and Epiphany if they fall on one of these days. One can say that two-thirds of the year is spent in fasting.

By fasting is meant abstinence from all animals and animal by-products. Only vegetables are allowed. Fasting is at least until midday, depending on the age and health of the person involved. In monasteries fasting is until sunset.

***

The Ethiopian Orthodox Church

Historical background

This church, sometimes called the Abyssinian Church, is closely related to the Coptic Church, as it shares the same early history. The exact date of the arrival of Christianity in Ethiopia is not certain, but we know that St Athanasius consecrated St Frumentius in about 347 as head of the Ethiopian Church. This was indicative of the fact that the Ethiopian Church came under the jurisdiction of Alexandria.

In the thirteenth century the Coptic Patriarch in Alexandria assumed the right to consecrate a Coptic bishop as metropolitan of the Ethiopian Church. Moreover Alexandria limited their episcopate to seven, thus effectively preventing them having their own metropolitan. This custom continued until 1959, when Emperor Haile Selassie I secured the autonomy of the Ethiopian Church. Henceforth they had a head known as a Catholicos-patriarch instead of the Coptic *abuna*. Their patriarch, Merkorios, resides in Addis Ababa. Although the primacy of Alexandria is acknowledged, the Ethiopian Church is independent in all things.

In 1626 they became Uniats (accepted the pope in Rome as their pope) under Jesuit influence, but when the Jesuits were expelled in the the year 1632, they reverted to their Coptic allegiance and so-called monophysitism. In fact, as a church they reject the term monophysite, preferring the term which translates as "unionite", expressing the union in Christ of the human and divine natures. They regard both Nestorius and Eutyches as heretics. At the time of the Council of Florence they rejected the agreed-upon union with Rome. Today they have become in some ways an "island" church in their isolation, with the Ethiopian Evangelical Mekane Yesus (EECMY) Church their main competitor. This latter has Lutheran contacts and support.

About 17 million in Ethiopia belong to this church.

Church life

Although it has much in common with other Orthodox churches, there are some aspects which are worthy of note. There are in the Ethiopian Church certain Judaizing tendencies, for example, the observance of the Sabbath, circumcision, and the distinction that is made between clean and unclean foods.

Among their practices, some of which are seen as superstitious and magical, the Virgin Mary is held in high esteem, some would say she is even divinized.

Their clergy consists of parish clergy and monks. The monks are seen as the true spiritual leaders of the people. The parish clergy on the other hand, consist of poorly educated or illiterate priests supported by lay clerks who are classified as part of the clergy.

In spite of coming within the jurisdiction of Alexandria for many centuries, the Ethiopian Church has preserved its own indigenous language (Ge'ez—a dead language since the sixteenth century), literature, art and music. Their worship is enlivened by the extensive use of drums and liturgical dances.

Their sacraments seem to have undergone change over the centuries. Baptism is done by triple immersion. Confirmation and the anointing of the sick are no longer practised. Penance/confession is still used but generally for deathbed cases.

***

Malankara Syrian Orthodox Church of India

Historical background

This church traces its origin to the Apostle St Thomas. When the Portuguese discovered India in the fifteenth century, there were about 100,000 St Thomas Christians in India. Over the centuries they had managed to maintain a measure of contact with the patriarch in Babylon/Baghdad, and had had a succession of bishops, all of whom came from Mesopotamia. Only in the seventeenth century did they get an indigenous Indian as bishop. The language of the liturgy was traditionally in Syriac.

Technically the Malankara Church, which does not accept the Council of Chalcedon, is a so-called monophysite church, but, as we have seen, these labels can be misleading and are often rejected by the people on whom they are pinned. Whatever the historical events, the Malankara Church is currently dialoguing with the Eastern Orthodox churches and the Roman Catholic Church. The latter dialogue began in 1989. The hope of these dialogues is that they will clear up the misunderstandings which originated with the often difficult Christological debates in the fourth and fifth centuries and for which many people and churches have suffered injustices over the centuries.

The current Catholicos (patriarch) or Catholicos Patriarch, of the Malankara Church is His Holiness Baselius Mar Thoma Mattheus II, Catholicos of the East. He resides in Kottayam, in the state of Kerala, India. The patron of this church is St Thomas, the Apostle.

Church life

The Malankara Church has seven sacraments: baptism, holy muron (chrism), eucharist, confession, holy matrimony, priesthood, and unction.

The liturgy of St James is used on big feast-days like Easter and Christmas. The liturgical calendar of the Malankara Church shares major feast-days with the West. Some, however, are not so well known in the West and rather peculiar to the Malankara Church, such as: the Sunday before Palm Sunday is Church Day, or "Catholicate" day; Good Friday is known as "Big Friday" followed by "Good News Saturday"; 3 July is St Thomas day, when the holy relics of St Thomas were taken to Odessa and installed there. The more important feast-day for St Thomas (his martyrdom) is actually 21 December; 15 August, called the Assumption in the West, is the feast of the Dormition of Our Holy Mother; 2 November is the feast of an Indian saint, Mar Gregorius. Great Lent starts on the Sunday after All Souls Day.

As regards fasting, Wednesdays and Fridays are fast days when fish may be eaten, but no other animal product. These laws apply in the period of Lent and Nineveh (three days' fast to commemorate the prophet Jonah and the Ninevites; it also commemorates the death of a tyrant king who died on the third day after the Catholicos of Babylon declared a fast). Concessions are made for special cases such as the old, sick, or pregnant women.

***

Syrian Orthodox Church

Historical background

This is one of the most ancient churches in Christendom. St Peter preached at Antioch before he ever got to Rome! At Antioch, where the patriarch used to reside, believers were first called Christians. Now the patriarch resides in Damascus. (The Antiochian Orthodox Church also has its patriarch resident in Damascus.)

They are sometimes called Jacobite after a sixth century archbishop, Jacob (James) Baradaeus. They were suppressed and deprived of their clergy by the Emperor Justinian, but revived under the favor of the Empress Theodora. Baradaeus marked the revival. They are in communion with the Copts, Ethiopians and Armenians.

For economic reasons (mainly), but also because of the different kinds of oppression they have suffered, there has been a diaspora of Syrians to all parts of the world. This has occurred mainly since 1945.

Church life

The non-acceptance of the Council of Chalcedon (451) is one distinguishing feature of this church. It accepts three ecumenical councils. Its members are called monophysite as a result, but incorrectly so, the way they see it. They maintain that the incarnated Word of God has one person not two, and one compound nature without confusion or mixture or change, since Jesus is true God and perfect man. His mother was *Theotokos* or God-bearer.

Their liturgy is celebrated in classical Syriac (whereas the Antiochians use Arabic). Priests in this church may marry but cannot become bishops unless their spouse dies. Currently bishops and archbishops come from the pool of celibate monks.

They see value in churches coming together, especially to resist the pressure of the reformed proselytising Churches.

***

Assyrian Church of the East

The Assyrian Church of the East is strictly speaking *not* one of the Oriental Orthodox churches because it has its own distinctive origin. It is included here because it is often associated with them.

Historical background

The history of this church, sometimes called the Holy Apostolic Catholic Assyrian Church of the East, is long and involved. It dates back to the first century. The church was within the Persian Empire and therefore remained unaffected by the many theological disputes, schisms and heresies that in later centuries arose within the imperial Christianity of the Roman Empire. According the the Assyrians, their church has no connection with the Councils of Ephesus and Chalcedon and had no representation at them. The Assyrian Church held its first synod in 410 under the patriarchate of Mar Issaq.

The church is not Nestorian, but in spite of this, authors like Henry Chadwick and Rouse and Neill refer to it as Nestorian: "Heresies of the 5th century remain to the present. The ancient 'Lesser' churches of the East—Coptic, Ethiopian, Syrian, Armenian, Assyrian—are all to this day either 'monophysite' or 'Nestorian'".[1] The Assyrian Church teaches the two natures in Christ.

Current research seems to suggest that Nestorius was frequently misrepresented and that Cyril was less correct than he has been presented in histories up to now. (Nestorius was bishop of Constantinople which was far removed from the diocese of Seleucia-Ctesephon, or Cteseiphon, in Babylon, which was later called Khurky or Kokhe, in the vicinity of Baghdad now in the country of Iraq.)

The Church of the East, as it was then, rejected the Council of Ephesus but did not reject Chalcedon. It does however reject the title "Mother of God" (*Theotokos*) preferring, "Mary Mother of Christ, our God". The Assyrian Church of the East does not use the term *Theotokos*. It holds that the term has no scriptural authority and is liable to misunderstanding. But the church gives the Virgin Mary her legitimate and deserving place. It calls her, the ever virgin, the Second Heaven, the Arc of Light, the mother of light and life, the mother of the Son of God, the mother of the Messiah, the mother of Emmanuel and the mother of our Lord, and Mary, mother of Christ our God.

In 1555 there was a split over the succession to the patriarchal See of Baghdad (Seleucia-Cteseiphon). The Synod made a decision and the losing candidate formed his own church, the Chaldean Church of the East. This church is now in union with Rome, but really is a sister church of the Assyrian Church of the East.

The Assyrians were expelled by their Muslim compatriots from Iraq after World War I and partly annihilated. In 1918 the Patriarch Mar Benyamin Shimmon was assassinated. His successor Mar Eshai Shimmon was expelled to Cyprus thence to England and finally was assassinated in California in 1975.

The present patriarch is H. H. Mar Dinkha IV, Catholicos Patriarch of the East, presently living in the USA. Currently there is an archdiocese in Iraq and a diocese in Baghdad, an archdiocese in India and Lebanon, and Europe. There are also two dioceses in the USA (East and West) and one each in Canada and Australia, with the dioceses of Syria and Iran under the jurisdiction of the Catholicos Patriarch.

Church life

Priests may marry, but not bishops. They used to have deaconesses but this practice stopped in the thirteenth century. Lack of priestly training is a big problem for this church. The monasteries and with them, their learning, have disappeared this century with all the fighting in northern Iraq. Currently candidates with two or three years preparation are ordained. There have been talks with the Vatican about candidates going to Catholic seminaries or universities. They desperately need to train theologians in their church.

They have seven sacraments: priesthood, baptism, anointing, holy eucharist, forgiveness of sins, holy leaven, and the sign of the cross. Religious education takes place mainly in Sunday schools.

Ecumenically the Assyrian Church of the East feels closest to the Roman Catholics and has a tight hierarchical system under the Catholicos Patriarch of Seleucia-Cteseiphon (presently Baghdad) who lives temporarily in the USA. He has the power to intervene in any diocese. Ordination of women is not practised.

***

Note
1. S. Neill and R. Rouse (eds.), *A History of the Ecumenical Movement*, London, SPCK, 1953, p. 12.

APPENDIX D

The Rites within the Roman Catholic Church

There are four main traditions or rites that date back to the earliest times in Christianity, reflecting the places to which it spread from Jerusalem. They are the *Roman* (Rome), *Antiochene* (Antioch), *Alexandrian* (Alexandria) and *Byzantine* (Constantinople) rites. From Antioch, Christianity spread to Armenia and what is now Iraq, so we add the *Armenian* and the *Chaldean* rites.

These rites, except for the Roman, are Eastern in character, have their own liturgies, languages, saints, feast-days and tend to celebrate the sacraments according to their own customs, for example, baptism and confirmation are usually given together, communion is by both species, or the bread dipped in the wine. Rite therefore refers to a total way of the Christian life; it refers to worship, canon law, asceticism and a particular theological system.

When the word "rite" is used in this comprehensive way, the Easterners prefer the word "church" to "rite". These "churches" are the uniat churches mentioned earlier in Chapter Two. But as we know the title "uniat church" offends the Orthodox churches! A further complication relates to the heading of this Appendix, "rites within the Roman Catholic Church". The uniat churches see themselves as part of the Catholic Church, not the *Roman* Catholic Church, the title of which seems to favour one church/rite within that body! I have stuck to the title Roman Catholic Church throughout this book since, rightly or wrongly, it is the official name for this church in ecumenical debate.

The list of rites follows below.

The Roman Tradition

There is one main rite in this Western tradition, known as the Latin rite, and four small rites known as the Ambrosian (Milan, Italy), Mozarabic (Toledo, Spain), Slavonic and Gallican (Lyons, France).

The *Latin* rite is centred on Rome and then Western Europe from whence it spread to the Western world. The language used in the liturgy was Latin and is now the vernacular. 98% of Roman Catholics belong to this rite.

Antiochene tradition

There are three rites: Maronite, Syrian and Malankara.

The *Maronite* rite honours St Maroun and St Chabel in particular. Originally from Lebanon, the languages used in the liturgy are Arabic, Aramaic and English. Their patriarch resides in Lebanon.

The *(West) Syrian* rite gives special honour to Saints Ephrem, Elias and Ignatius of Antioch. Aramaic and Arabic are the languages of the liturgy. The followers of the Syrian rite live in the countries of the Middle East, but like the others, some have emigrated to the New World. Their patriarch lives in Lebanon.

The *Malankara* rite in India uses Malayalam as a liturgical language.

East Syrian (Chaldean) tradition

There are two rites: the Chaldean and the Malabar rites.

The *Chaldean* rite is found in Iraq and they use Aramaic in their liturgies. The saints that originally brought Christianity to them were Saints Thomas, Addai, Agai and Mari. Their patriarch lives in Iraq. Its sister church, which is not in communion with Rome, is the Assyrian

Church of the East. Their followers have emigrated to all parts of the world such as the USA, Canada, Australia and New Zealand.

The *Malabar* rite is found in India and uses Malayalam as its liturgical language.

Armenian tradition

There is only one rite.

The *Armenian* rite uses classical Armenian in its liturgy as well as French and English. Originally from Armenia, they are now in the Middle East and in the USA and Australia. St Gregory the Illuminator and St Vartan and martyrs are their best known saints. Their patriarch resides in Lebanon.

Alexandrian tradition

There are two rites: the Coptic and Ethiopic rites.

The *Coptic* rite originated in Egypt. St Mark is said to be their founder but they also honour St Anthony of Egypt. Their liturgy, celebrated in white hood and alb, is that of St Basil and their languages are Coptic and Arabic. Cairo is the home of the Coptic Patriarch. Christmas is celebrated on 7 January.

The *Ethiopic* rite, found in Ethiopia, uses Ge'ez (now a dead language) in its liturgies which are strongly influenced by African music, handclapping and dancing.

Byzantine tradition

There are nine rites as follows.

The *Melkite* rite is found in Middle Eastern countries like Lebanon, Egypt, Syria and Israel, with a patriarch in Damascus. Greek is its liturgical language. The main liturgy is that of St John Chrysostom.

The *Ukrainian* rite uses the Ukrainian language mainly in its liturgy. Christianity came to the Ukraine in 988. Saints Vladimir and Cyril and

Methodius are the popular saints. Their elected cardinal resides in Rome. Ukrainians have emigrated to countries like the USA, Canada and Australia.

The *Russian* rite uses old Slavonic and some English in its liturgy, depending on where it is found in the world. They have emigrated to China, Europe, North America and Australia. Like the Ukrainians, they claim St Vladimir as their patron and list Saints Olga and Nicholas among their favourites. Their elected bishop resides in Rome.

The *Bulgarian* rite uses Bulgarian in its liturgies and has been in existence since 863, when Photius, the Patriarch of Constantinople, introduced Boris I into Christianity.

The *Greek* rite uses Greek in its liturgies and was established in 1856.

The *Georgian* rite uses the liturgies of both St Basil and St John Chrysostom, and the Georgian language.

The *Italo-Albanian* rite, found in Southern Italy, Sicily, Malta and Corsica uses both Greek and Albanian as liturgical languages.

The *Romanian* rite, united with Rome since 1698, uses Romanian in its liturgies.

The *Serbian* rite uses Slavonic.

Some classifications go further and add seven more rites, or sub-rites to this list, namely, *Albanian, Byelorussian, Hungarian, Ruthenian, Slovak, Yugoslav* and *USA*.

List of Church Councils

No.	Year(s)	Name of Council (Issue(s) dealt with)
	50	Council of Jerusalem (Jewish laws & Christians)
1	325	1st Council of Nicaea (contra Arianism;[1] Creed)
2	381	1st Council of Constantinople (completed Creed)
3	432	Council of Ephesus (contra Nestorianism[2])
4	451	Council of Chalcedon (contra Monophysitism;[3] stated principle of the hypostatic union[4])
5	553	2nd Council of Constantinople (contra Nestorians)
6	681	3rd Council of Constantinople (contra Monothelitism[5])
7	767	2nd Council of Nicaea (veneration of images legal) (The first 7 are recognized as Ecumenical Councils by the Orthodox.)
8	869	4th Council of Constantinople (East-West peace) (The first 8 are recognized as Ecumenical Councils by Roman Catholics.)

No.	Year(s)	Name of Council (Issue(s) dealt with)
9	1123	1st Lateran Council (discipline; contra Waldensians & Albigenses)
10	1139	2nd Lateran Council (as previous)
11	1179	3rd Lateran Council (as previous)
12	1215	4th Lateran Council (as previous)
13	1245	1st Council of Lyons
14	1274	2nd Council of Lyons
15	1311	Council of Vienne
16	1414–18	Council of Constance (ended rival popes)
17	1431–43	Basle-Ferrara-Florence-Lausanne (reform and union with Eastern churches)
18	1512–17	5th Lateran Council
19	1545–63	Council of Trent (reform)
20	1870	1st Vatican Council (doctrine of papal infallibility)
21	1962–5	2nd Vatican Council (adaptation of Church to modern needs)

Notes

1. Denial of Christ's divinity.
2. Heresy that Mary was mother of Christ's humanity, not his divinity, hence it rejected the title *Theotokos* (Mother of God).
3. Belief in only one nature in Christ.
4. The union of a human and divine nature in the one person of Christ.
5. Heresy of only one will in Christ.

GLOSSARY

Autocephalous: Independent, self-governing; used of churches that are self-governing and appoint their own chief bishop.

Canonical: According to church law; valid in the eyes of the Church.

Catholicism: That body of Christianity which acknowledges the pope as its spiritual leader.

Catholicos: The patriarch or head bishop of some Oriental Orthodox churches, such as the Armenian or Malankara Syrian Orthodox churches. His area of supervision is known as his Catholicosate or Catholicate.

Christology: The study of the person, life and works of Jesus Christ.

Communicatio in sacris: Sharing in the sacraments; it usually refers to the full eucharistic sharing between and among separated Christians.

Conciliar: Refers to a council, e.g., conciliar authority refers to the authority of a council.

Covenant: An agreement between people or groups, especially between Christian churches wanting to collaborate or promote ecumenism.

Ecclesiology: From the Latin, *ecclesia*, meaning Church; the study of the Church, or the theory and nature of the Church.

Ecumenical: Pertaining to ecumenism; thus ecumenical services, or ecumenical perspectives.

Ecumenism: The movement of Christians towards unity.

Eparchy: The Eastern term equivalent to a Western diocese.

Exarch: The representative of a patriarch.

Filioque: The Latin for "from the Son". It was a clause inserted into the Nicean Creed in the West without the agreement of the Eastern Church.

Fundamentalism: The tendency to interpret Scripture very literally; as regards doctrine it indicates extreme conservatism.

Heresy: An incorrect teaching; a teaching or doctrine held not to be in agreement with accepted doctrine.

Iconostasis: The screen, covered in icons, which separates the sanctuary from the nave in Orthodox churches.

Indulgence: The remission of a temporal punishment due to forgiven sins in virtue of the merits of Christ; granted under special conditions.

Interchurch: Involving two or more churches, usually Christian churches.

Intercommunion: See *communicatio in sacris.*

Interfaith: Involving two or more world religions, e.g., Christians and Jews, or Hindus and Muslims.

Irenicism: The state and love of peace or pacifism.

Koinonia: Means communion or fellowship of Christians.

Mainline: Refers to the largest and oldest Christian churches.

Mariology: The systematic study of Mary and her place in the story of salvation.

Monophysite: Literally, one nature; it refers to those Christians who believed that Christ had one nature, not two as the Council of Chalcedon taught.

Orthodoxy: That expression of Eastern Christianity which dates from the East–West Schism of 1054, and in the case of some churches, even earlier.

Patriarch: The spiritual leader or head bishop of a group of Christians.

Primacy: Being first; the bishop of Rome is said to have a position of primacy among his fellow bishops.

Proselytism: The action of attempting to win over members of another religious group to one's own church by disreputable means.

Proselytize: The act that is done to result in proselytism.

Protestant Episcopal Church: That American denomination whose heritage derives from the reformed Church of England.

Protestantism: That expression of Christianity which takes its origin from the sixteenth century Continental Reformation; it has become very diverse in its beliefs and practices.

Reception: The act of the local church in accepting the ecumenical decisions or agreements of church leaders.

Reformation: The movement in history which gave rise to the new Christian churches in the sixteenth century in Europe.

Reformed: Refers to those churches in Switzerland and their descendants that reformed their Christianity at the time of the Reformation in a more thorough way than the Lutherans. Today they are called the Reformed churches.

Rite: The Roman Catholic Church is said to have rites within the church. It is a style of Christian life of a community; it refers to worship, canon law, asceticism and to a particular theological system.

Schism: A breach of charity and love, not one of doctrine, between people or groups in a church, which results in a breakaway group or groups.

Sectarianism: Strong adherence to a religious group or church with strong feelings of intolerance against other factions or churches.

Simony: The buying and selling of religious or spiritual benefits.

Transubstantiation: The explanation, dating from Medieval times, of how Christ was present in the bread and wine in the eucharist. The 'substance' of the bread and wine is said to change into the body and blood of Christ, while the 'accidents' of bread and wine remain.

Uniat(e): A Christian rite/church not belonging to a Latin patriarchate but in union with, and submitting to the authority of, the Roman papacy.

Uniatism: The tendency or movement of Eastern churches to unite with Rome. Churches which have already done so are called Uniat churches.

Usury: Interest charged on money lent. Today simply referred to as interest.

BIBLIOGRAPHY

Abrecht, P. & R. Shinn (eds), *Faith and Science in an Unjust World*, Vols I & II, Geneva, WCC, 1980.

Arruda, M. (ed.), *Ecumenism and the New World Order: The Failure of the 1970's and the Challenges of the 1980's*, Geneva, WCC, 1980.

Avis, P., *Christians in Communion*, London, Mowbray & Geoffrey Chapman, 1990.

Aveling, J. et al. (eds), *Rome and the Anglicans*, New York, Gruyter, 1982.

Barrett, D. (ed), *World Christian Encyclopedia*, Nairobi & London, OUP, 1982.

Best, T. F. (ed.), *Living Today: Towards Visible Unity*, Fifth International Consultation of United and Uniting Churches, Faith and Order Paper No. 142, Geneva, WCC, 1988.

Bilheimer, R., *Breakthrough: The Emergence of the Ecumenical Tradition*, Geneva, WCC, 1989.

Bluck, J., *Canberra Take Aways*, Risk Book Series, Geneva, WCC, 1991.

Bokenkotter, T., *A Concise History of the Catholic Church*, New York, Doubleday, 1977.

Boyd, R., *Ireland: Christianity Discredited or Pilgrim's Progress?*, Risk Book Series, Geneva, WCC, 1988.

Bria, I., *The Sense of Ecumenical Tradition: The Ecumenical Witness and Vision of the Orthodox*, Geneva, WCC, 1991.

British Council of Churches, *Views from the Pews*, London, BCC, 1986.

Brown, R. et al., *Peter in the New Testament*, Minneapolis, Paulist Press, 1973.

Butler, B., *The Church and Unity*, London, Chapman, 1979.

Clark, S., *Building Christian Communities*, Notre Dame, Ave Maria Press, 1972.

Congar, Y., *Dialogue Between Christians*, London, Chapman, 1966.

_____ *Diversity and Communion*, London, SCM, 1984.

_____ *Fifty Years of Catholic Theology*, London, SCM, 1988.

Dalmais, I-H., *The Eastern Liturgies*, trans. by D. Attwater, London, Burns and Oates, 1960.

Daton, D. (ed.), *Breaking Barriers: Nairobi 1975*, London, SPCK, 1976.

Derr, T., *Barriers to Ecumenism*, New York, Orbis Books, 1983.

Desseaux, J., *Twenty Centuries of Ecumenism*, trans. by M. O'Connell, New York, Paulist Press, 1991.

Ellis, C., *Together On The Way: A Theology of Ecumenism*, London, British Council of Churches, 1990.

Finn, E., *These Are My Rites*, Collegeville, Liturgical Press, 1980.

Flint, E., *Family of Believers*, Dayton, Pflaum, 1969.

Gillman, I., *Many Faiths One Nation*, Sydney, Collins, 1988.

Hayes, V., *We Came Together: A Popular Report on Evanston*, Melbourne, Wilkie, 1954.

Hurley, M., *The Theology of Ecumenism*, Cork, Mercier, 1969.

Huxtable, J., *A New Hope for Christian Unity*, Glasgow, Collins, 1979

Johnson, D. (ed.), *Uppsala to Nairobi*, London, SPCK, 1975.

Keshishian, A., *Conciliar Fellowship: A Common Goal*, Geneva, WCC, 1992.

Limouris, G., *Justice, Peace and the Integrity of Creation: Insights from Orthodoxy*, Geneva, WCC, 1990.

Lossky, N. et al. (eds), *Dictionary of the Ecumenical Movement*, Geneva, WCC, Grand Rapids, Eerdmans, 1991.

Mackie, S. (ed.), *Can Churches be Compared?*, New York, Friendship Press, 1970.

Nichols, A., *Rome and the Eastern Churches*, Edinburgh, T. & T. Clark, 1992.

Niles, P., *Resisting the Threat to Life: Covenanting for Justice, Peace and the Integrity of Creation*, Risk Book Series, Geneva, WCC, 1989.

Raiser, K., *Ecumenism in Transition: A Paradigm Shift in the Ecumenical Movement?*, Geneva, WCC, 1991.

Rouse, R. & S. Neill (eds), *A History of the Ecumenical Movement*, London, SPCK, 1953.

Samartha, S. (ed.), *Towards World Community*, Geneva, WCC, 1975.

Tillard, J., *The Bishop of Rome*, Delaware, Michael Glazier, 1983.

Tomkins, O., *A Time for Unity*, London, SCM, 1964.

Van der Bent, Ans J., *Vital Ecumenical Concerns: Sixteen Documentary Surveys*, Geneva, WCC, 1986.

Van Elderen, M., *Introducing the World Council of Churches*, revised edition, Risk Book Series, Geneva, WCC, 1992.

Wainwright, G., *The Ecumenical Moment: Crisis and Opportunity for the Church*, Grand Rapids, Eerdmans, 1983.

Wieser, T. (ed.), *Whither Ecumenism? A Dialogue in the Transit Lounge of the Ecumenical Movement*, Geneva, WCC, 1986.

World Council of Churches, *Confessing The One Faith*, new revised version, Faith and Order Paper No. 153, Geneva, WCC, 1991.

INDEX